SUPERPOWERS FOR GOOD

The Skills You Can Master to Leave Your Mark on the World

by

DEVIN D. THORPE

Superpowers for Good
The Skills You Can Master to Leave Your Mark on the World

For the changemakers

Acknowledgments

Although I sat down to write this book just 90 days ago, I started work on it years ago, when I began asking podcast guests, "What is your superpower?" Their answers have enriched me.

I'm grateful to Angel Matos, who I credit with first having the idea of compiling the inspirational answers into a book.

The people profiled in this book gave generously of their time to be interviewed at least once and sometimes twice. They also provided written background materials and responded to written questions. I cannot thank them enough.

There were too many qualified answers to include them all, so I want to recognize the value that all my podcast guests had in preparing this book. Hundreds of people answered that question. I wish I could have included them all.

For nearly a decade, I employed a couple, Chandon Saha and Api Podder, who helped manage a frantically prolific collection of three websites to which we (they) posted content almost 365 days per year. We suspended that work at the end of 2019. Before we wrapped up our work together, they helped me organize this book's interviews, transcripts, and recordings. I couldn't have done it without them.

Jae Varela is a writer and editor based in Salt Lake City. She has edited several of my books and many for others, on my recommendation. Jae did a fabulous job editing this book almost in real-time as I wrote it, enabling me to move immediately from writing to promoting. She made every page better.

Gail, my wife of 33 years, was the first reader and reviewer. As a retired school teacher, she is qualified to get out the red pen and mark errors. Instead, she used every chapter as an opportunity to encourage me to keep going. I derive my superpowers entirely from her.

Notwithstanding all the help I've received in so many ways, any errors you find in this book are mine alone.

Message From the Author

This book is collection of insights from proven changemakers who shared their superpowers in recorded interviews for my podcast. You can subscribe to the "Superpowers for Good" podcast and newsletter at superpowers4good.com.

A list of all the links in the book can be found at http://list.s4g.biz.

Table of Contents

Introduction

Several years ago, after doing about 800 episodes of my podcast, I started asking guests a consistent question: "What is your superpower?" I even got to put the question to Bill Gates.

The quirky question frequently caught guests off guard just enough to evoke fascinating responses. Then something intriguing happened. People started commenting to me about the question and the answers.

More than two years ago, I began work on compiling some of the most profound responses—and the answers from some of the most interesting people—for this book. I set it aside to spend 2020 in a failed bid for a seat in Congress.

After licking my wounds for a time, I picked up where I'd left off. As I read my guests' answers and began writing about their insights and examples, I realized I was learning. A lot. They inspired me. I can't wait to read and reread this book to soak in the wisdom of extraordinary people.

Are they superheroes? They are no more superheroes than patience or optimism are literal superpowers. With this book, I don't want to encourage a white savior mentality. I've seen that guy. Painfully, I should admit, I've been that guy.

For the past decade, I've worked to align my journalistic writing—much of it for Forbes—with the principles of solutions-oriented journalism, which focuses on repeatable efforts that provide measurable relief to social and environmental problems. This dogma holds that there are no heroes, examining the processes and tools rather than the people wielding them.

Here's the thing. Over and over again, I found the people were essential to the processes. How do you remove Bill Gates from a story about the Gates Foundation? He isn't a savior. He isn't a Marvel superhero. There are, however, things we can learn from him.

1

There are also powerful and vital lessons we can learn from the BIPOC women profiled in the book. More than half the people profiled are women—amazing, inspiring examples everyone can learn from.

Years ago, I wrote a book called *Your Mark on the World.* The reality is we focus too much on our legacy and not enough on the problems facing others and how we can help eliminate them. However, if solving problems and serving others comes from a desire to leave a legacy, I'm inclined to celebrate rather than chasten.

Kimmy Paluch, a venture capitalist profiled in Chapter 49, shared some thoughts about her legacy with me.

"I'm proud of all of my achievements, but I hold a much higher bar for what comes next," she explained. "Do I use it for my own gratification or my own self-interests, or do I pay it forward?" she asks. "When your goals are much bigger than yourself, you will have a lot more to be proud of."

So, please, think about the mark you leave on the world and use that to motivate your service to others.

Many, perhaps most, of the people I ask about superpowers first deny having them. One implication is that humility is a largely unacknowledged superpower that is common among people focused on changemaking. That makes them more worthy of emulation.

Another common theme that is observably true is that many people in the book noted that their superpower was a double-edged sword and was both a blessing and a curse. A tenacious person can persevere through challenges others cannot but may also be reluctant to quit when ahead or to give up when the game is over. Superpowers are traits and skills we learn to manage and optimize.

As you read the book, think about your strengths. Identify the superpowers you most closely align with. Work to build on those. No one has all 60. Most people have just one or two that are truly defining. That is true even of the most accomplished people in the book. Don't feel like you need to focus on having dozens.

If you recognize, however, that you have a success-limiting shortcoming, see if you can pick up enough from related superpowers to overcome the weakness. Don't worry about owning such powers; just learn enough to allow you to move forward unimpeded.

As you consider each superpower, you'll notice that many are interrelated. As you build patience, you give yourself more time to gain other strengths as well. As you learn problem-solving skills, you'll enhance your optimism. If you got business training in the 90s, you'll recognize the concept of synergy here.

Because every superpower discussed could help you, consider reading just one chapter per day. You'll finish in about two months. You may want to review the book one chapter per week after reading it once to further reflect on how you can strengthen your abilities to serve others.

Before you launch into the rest of the book, it is worth noting that no one paid for inclusion. The people in the book didn't know I would include them until after I made that decision. That said, I've done business with a few of the people profiled. Some paid for travel associated with stories I wrote years ago, sponsored my podcast or supported my Congressional campaign. I included no one for any reason other than being relevant.

As a former(?) politician, I should also note that I did not screen the people included in the book for their political affiliation. In most cases, I have no idea how they vote. Some live and work outside the U.S. Bottom line: this is not a book about politics.

Now, go find and master the superpowers you'll use to leave your mark on the world.

.

Part I: Altruism

Among the 66 people featured in this book for their superpowers, 17 mentioned powers clustered around altruism. The people and their strengths are focused on other people, frequently on those they serve.

Katharine Hayhoe by Mark Umstot Photography

Chapter 1: Being Human - Katharine Hayhoe

Devin: *Katharine, what is your superpower?*

Katharine: *Probably a really good quality fish oil! I would say the only superpower really is being human and remembering that I'm human. We're so quick to draw the lines between people and say, well, I don't like you because... But if we can focus again on what we have in common, what unites us, what values we share—and that's something that I can't always do necessarily—but if we can do that, that is all of our superpowers.*

You can watch the full interview with Katharine here: <u>kat.s4g.biz</u>.

Katharine Hayhoe is among an elite group of climate scientists who have reached something approaching celebrity status for their ability to communicate with ordinary people. She is uniquely recognized as the voice of reason with climate change skeptics, especially those who share her Christian faith.

She hosts a YouTube show for PBS called "Global Weirding." (No, that is not a typo.) In the show, she explains how we don't perceive global warming—even though it is happening. Instead, we perceive weird weather, like massive storms that previously only happened once in 100 years, happening two or three times in a few years. That's what she calls global weirding.

She's a big deal. Her peers recognized her with the American Geophysical Union's climate communication prize and the Stephen Schneider Climate Communication award. Time Magazine named her among its 100 Most Influential People. Foreign Policy added her to its list of 100 Leading Thinkers. FORTUNE magazine included her on its list of the World's Greatest Leaders.

As an undergraduate, she studied astrophysics and planned to pursue that field as a graduate student until she took a course on climate change. She hadn't appreciated that this area of study was an extension of physics, the same work she'd been doing. She says she was also shocked to realize how global warming threatens not just the environment but people. A warming planet could harm everyone she cares about—everyone you care about.

If you care about poverty and social justice, you already care about climate change; you just may not know it yet. With that fresh perspective, recognizing that as a budding physicist, she had the foundational skills required to work in the field and that her work would help people around the world, Katharine knew she'd found her calling.

She went on to earn a Ph.D. in atmospheric science from the University of Illinois. She has also been awarded two honorary doctorates from Colgate University and Victoria University at the University of Toronto.

The Nature Conservancy recently tapped Katharine to serve as its Chief Scientist. Working from her home in Lubbock, Texas, she retains an appointment as a professor.

As I weigh her accomplishments and capabilities, it is easy to picture her wearing a cape and leaping tall buildings. Perhaps I should have expected her to name "being human" as her superpower, but I assumed something more along the lines of "superhuman communication skills."

Upon further reflection, however, I see how her humanness defines her. Her particular ability to connect with climate skeptics requires that she be able to empathize with them. Her foundation for empathy is in recognizing her own humanity. She acknowledges that since we are all human, we have much more in common than the stuff that divides us. From that position, she doesn't speak down to people. She speaks to them eye-to-eye. She respects them. In response, they hear her.

How to Develop Being Human as a Superpower

There are three Ms that can help you to make being human a superpower. Of course, you are human, so I don't intend these tips to make you human so much as to help you own your humanity.

Mortality

Not only is everyone you meet headed for the grave right along with you, but they are also experiencing the other challenges that life constantly serves up. If you assume that everyone you meet is going through the emotional equivalent of a job loss, death in the family or divorce, you'll be right often enough.

By noting your shared mortality, you can be just a bit more patient and understanding with people who may disagree with you. You can find your inner Katharine.

Mistakes

Don't make more; just note that you do make mistakes. It is easy to look down on people who slip up when you see yourself as above that. Psychologists refer to this idea as the fundamental attribution error. Most people assume that the screw-ups others make are evidence of fundamental character flaws, and those we make ourselves result from mere expediency.

For instance, if someone cuts you off in traffic, you might think (or, if you're like me, shout), "what a jerk!" When you cut someone off in traffic, if you notice at all, you're likely to think it was required or at least justified by the circumstances. By recognizing this pattern, we can begin to offer others the same sort of compassion we give ourselves. It is worth noting some people who experience low self-esteem reverse the fundamental attribution error and need to treat themselves with the same generosity they've been treating others.

Modesty

With the word "modesty," I don't mean to suggest that your bathing suit should cover an adequate part of your body. If you want to rock that speedo, go for it! Instead, I mean to encourage humility.

Of course, the problem with being modest is that the moment you say you aspire to it, someone will answer that you've lost it. It is a semantic, if not a moral, trap.

You can, however, become more teachable. What is humility if it isn't the ability to acknowledge you have something to learn and then make an

9

effort to learn it? By seeing yourself as a learner, you take yourself off the pedestal you didn't even know you were standing on. Now you can speak to your fellow humans as peers.

By working on the three Ms, you celebrate your humanity, putting yourself on the same level as everyone else. With practice, it can become a superpower.

Joanne Chiwaula

Chapter 2: Being Inspired by Those You Work With and Serve - Joanne Chiwaula

Devin: *Well, Joanne, what is your superpower?*

Joanne: *I definitely don't have a superpower. I think, as I said, it's really just staying inspired by the people that I'm working with and working for. And I think when I go to Malawi, and I see the work that the nurses are doing, I feel so much pride, and I feel so much joy to see the connections between the nurses and these communities. That's not something that you typically see between health care workers and patients. Health care workers typically are very overworked, very stressed and seeing maybe 80 patients in a day. Just to see their families laughing and chatting and this banter that they have, and the exchange and then the gratitude and the affection—also, seeing that in the nurses, which I also haven't seen previously in the hospitals in Malawi, that they also feel fulfilled in the work that they're doing. That just gives me so much inspiration. And then I come back like OK, we've got to do this—got to make it bigger. So, that's the source of the energy.*

You can watch the full interview with Joanne here: joanne.s4g.biz.

Joanne Chiwaula is a certified nurse-midwife and women's nurse practitioner who founded the nonprofit African Mothers Health Initiative (AMHI) to help vulnerable babies and women in Malawi. With an undergraduate degree in international studies from Brown University and a master's degree from the University of California at San Francisco, she is exceptionally well educated. She is a professional.

Early in her career, she worked for three years in Malawi at a hospital where 1,000 babies were delivered every month. While there, she learned about a tragic phenomenon. Babies born to mothers who don't survive childbirth or die soon after face a mortality rate of 80 percent. Local custom concludes that babies just want to be with their mothers.

Joanne began personally following up with these babies, visiting them in their homes and communities, educating people on the babies' care and helping to provide formula. Then, before moving to Ghana, she organized local nurses to do what she'd started.

She saw how quickly the local women were able to replicate and improve upon what she'd started. She then organized AMHI in the United States to raise money for the program in Malawi.

Now, 15 years later, hundreds of mothers and babies are in the program. The babies include the orphans and other vulnerable ones, including multiple births with higher mortality rates, partly because low-income mothers may not be getting meals regularly enough to nurse two or three children.

AMHI has a program for women if they've had a complicated delivery or lost a baby. A challenging delivery may result in losing her ability to have more children. Families or communities may shun women who've lost a baby or their uterus. The nurses now visit the women to educate their neighbors and families, dispel myths and rumors that lead to shunning and help women create incomes that provide security and confidence if other resources fail.

The program is dramatically successful, reducing infant mortality in these high-risk situations by up to two-thirds.

Though Joanne doesn't see it as a superpower, the people she works with and serves inspire her to keep going. At first blush, this seems easy to believe and emulate, but many, if not most, people who help other people professionally sometimes tire of the interactions and their demands. Who hasn't complained to a friend outside the office about a colleague's behavior? Joanne's example is crucial for us to understand.

How to Develop Being Inspired by Those You Work With and Serve as a Superpower

To better understand her superpower and how you can emulate it, I visited with Joanne again. You can watch my second interview with her here: joanne2.s4g.biz.

Joanne shared an inspiring story to help us understand what she's saying.

One of the women who graduated from the AMHI program recently shared with Joanne how she got involved. A friend of hers had passed away, and when she attended the funeral, she discovered the friend had left a baby.

"And she saw the baby who was just a couple of days old, and she saw people diluting a soda. And she said, 'Who is that drink for?' And they said, 'This is for the baby.' She said, 'No, you can't give that soda to the baby,'" Joanne reports.

The friends with the baby suggested that she take the baby and find an NGO in town that would feed and care for the baby. The woman took the baby but couldn't find an NGO to help, so she returned with the baby. Hours later, the baby, carried by her sister, arrived at the woman's home. The girl explained that the family and community had decided they couldn't care for the baby, "You keep the baby and keep looking for an NGO."

The woman, a mother of five, now had another mouth to feed. Finally, her husband said, "I don't want this nonsense in my house. If you're going to take care of this baby, you need to find a different place to live."

Courageously, the woman concluded that the baby would not die on her watch, so she took the baby and began looking for someone to provide milk or formula. Finally, someone at a health center directed her to AMHI. The nurses there helped her and the baby for two years. That baby is now a healthy toddler.

"So, if she can do that, if she can say, 'This baby needs to survive, and I'm willing to sacrifice my entire life for the survival of this child,' I'm happy to share her story and do a little work trying to raise some money," Joanne says. "I feel like I don't have any other option. If she can do that, I can do my small part."

That is an inspiring story. Moreover, it hints at some critical lessons that Joanne shared.

1. *Be there.* To connect with your colleagues and the people you serve, you have to show up. Today that can include virtual participation, but you have to put in some time.
2. *Slow down.* The frenetic pace of 21st-century life distracts from the most important things. To make a connection, hear a story, and learn from those you serve, you have to slow down.

3. *Listen.* You'll learn more and build a stronger connection from listening than from talking. Ask open-ended questions. Paraphrase to ensure you understand.
4. *Be patient.* Some of the people you serve and work with have experienced trauma. Who knows what word, what question, what situation could trigger anxiety. Don't demand answers. Work to create a safe space for sharing and wait for it to come.
5. *Empower locals.* Joanne learned early on that local people could do better work serving people than she could. Nonetheless, she maintains a vital ongoing role as a fundraiser and spokesperson in the United States. Still, she recognizes that her role is to support the brilliant women doing the work in Malawi.
6. *Empathize.* Remember, Joanne says, that mothers in Malawi love their children as much as mothers elsewhere. It is tempting, she notes, to think that people surrounded by suffering somehow become immune to the pain. Not so. Mothers there suffer just as much when they lose a child.

If you seek inspiration from those you work with and serve, you'll find it. It's there. With that positive energy as a superpower, you can increase the good you're doing in the world.

Winnie Mpanju-Shumbusho

Chapter 3: Communication - Winnie Mpanju-Shumbusho

Devin: *Dr. Winnie, what is your superpower?*

Dr. Winnie: *That's an interesting question. I'm not sure what superpower is, Devin, but what I can say is it's the ability to be able to connect with people from all walks of life, to be able to deliver a message to them that allows them to see their role in whatever efforts we're trying, you know, to involve them, but also being able to simplify and demystify science for the ordinary person. I'm perfectly comfortable sitting under a tree in a village discussing malaria as I am sitting in the World Health Assembly talking about malaria. So for me, I find key ingredients to being successful in the battle against these deadly diseases.*

You can watch the full interview with Dr. Winnie here: winnie.s4g.biz.

Although far from a household name, Dr. Winnie Mpanju-Shumbusho is among the most accomplished people ever to have joined me on my show. She has been working to improve global public health throughout her career, which spans almost four decades.

In 2018, she joined a research project for the prestigious scientific journal, *The Lancet*, which made a case for the complete eradication of malaria.[1] It wasn't until 2015 that people working on malaria began to see that as a possibility. Her work has helped to clarify that the only acceptable goal for the disease is eradication.

The world needs complete eradication, partly because drug and insecticide resistance could make controlling the disease impossible in the future, potentially subjecting more people to malaria than now.

According to the World Health Organization, 400,000 people die annually from malaria, two-thirds of them children under five.[2]

Dr. Winnie's leadership is bringing the world closer to preventing those 400,000 annual deaths and the suffering that comes from the hundreds of millions of cases each year. Her career has also included work to address HIV/AIDS, tuberculosis and rare tropical diseases. The number of people whose lives have already been impacted by her work is almost inestimable. If anyone on the planet should be wearing a superhero cape, she should.

Consider Dr. Winnie's superpower. I've attached the label "communication" to her description. With all she knows about science and medicine, I find it fascinating that she considers her ability to communicate with a wide range of audiences, from the World Health Assembly to villagers sitting under a tree, to be her most impactful capability.

How to Develop Communication as a Superpower

While Dr. Winnie is well educated, with a collection of degrees earned in the United States and Tanzania, she didn't study communications. Everyone can learn to communicate better.

As an author, speaker, politician, podcaster and journalist, I've never had to communicate more effectively than I did in business. Effective communication is an essential skill for everyone in every role. Try to imagine a surgeon, programmer or plumber doing their work correctly without communicating meaningfully with their patients, clients, customers or colleagues.

Here are eight tips to help you learn to communicate more effectively.

1. *Be approachable.* Even when you are the expert, it is vital to convey an attitude or vibe of approachability—even vulnerability.

---

[1] The Lancet, "The Lancet Commission on malaria eradication," April 16, 2018, Ingrid Chen, Rebecca Cooney, Richard G A Feachem, Altaf Lal, Winnie Mpanju-Shumbusho, https://www.thelancet.com/journals/lancet/article/PIIS0140-6736(18)30911-5/fulltext
[2] World Health Organization, World Malaria Report 2020, https://www.who.int/teams/global-malaria-programme/reports/world-malaria-report-2020

Your audience will pay more attention if they are pulling for you to succeed.

2. *Have fun.* Whether writing or speaking, appearing to enjoy yourself and helping others to enjoy themselves will help you deliver your message. The most common way to have fun is to share an *appropriate* joke.

3. *Tell stories.* From the moment you begin a story, your audience—whether one or one thousand—will instantly connect to your message. Don't just tell stories to get their attention. Use them to make your points.

4. *Use P.I.P.* Introduce your topic by telling your audience the Purpose, the Importance and then giving a Preview of your message.

5. *Be succinct.* Whether writing or speaking, there is no extra credit for extra words. Say what you mean and move on.

6. *Know your audience.* Dr. Winnie doesn't deliver the same message to villagers sitting under a tree as she does when speaking to the World Health Assembly. She manifests the same respect for both audiences by addressing them and their concerns appropriately.

7. *Don't rely on visual aids.* Visual aids, including PowerPoint, can add to your ability to communicate. Just as often, however, they will distract. Know this: if you can't give your presentation without the visual aids, you don't know the material well enough. Try to delete all the words from your visual aids, using only photos to enhance your message.

8. *Speak extemporaneously.* In most circumstances, you will be most effective by speaking from an outline rather than a script. You should know the materials sufficiently well to deliver your message without reading or memorizing a script.

9. *Listen.* You cannot be an effective communicator without listening.

Even if you cannot make communication a superpower as Dr. Winnie has, you can do more good by learning to speak and write well.

Ennie Lim

Chapter 4: Connecting With People - Ennie Lim

Devin: *Ennie, what is your superpower?*

Ennie: *What is my superpower? I would have to say my ability to connect with people. I think that is really something that's brought us this far. It's a new program for a lot of people for allowing employers to understand what their employees are really going through.*

It's me going out there and sharing the story and my personal story and why it's important to, just for a second, just to feel what an employee might be going through or somebody that may look like they're doing well, but they could be going through a lot. So, that, I guess, would be my superpower.

You can watch the full interview with Ennie here: ennie.s4g.biz.

Ennie Lim is the CEO and founder of Honey Bee. This fintech firm helps employers provide small, short-term emergency loans or payday advances at fair, affordable rates. Comparable to credit card interest rather than the tenfold or more rates charged by payday lenders, employees and employers love the solution.

Most Americans don't have $500 of cash for an emergency. Those who don't have credit cards can quickly find themselves in financial trouble when a car or appliance repair suddenly appears.

Honey Bee secures the loans with the employee's paid time off balance accrued with the employer. If the employee leaves the company before the loan is completely repaid, the balance is deducted from the employee's PTO payout. The standard loan term is three months, with five bi-weekly installments beginning about 30 days after the employee borrows the money. The cost of a loan is 5 percent of the loan amount, but never more than $50. Loan amounts go up to $2,500.

Ennie notes that the borrowers are considered sub-prime. That is, credit rating agencies have cut their scores due to late payments. As a result, they are not eligible for credit cards or other affordable consumer loans. Honey Bee is thereby helping to restore and strengthen their credit scores.

In addition to the loan programs, Honey Bee also provides online financial education and counseling resources to employees of participating companies. Ennie focuses on helping people avoid financial problems caused by predatory lending. One-on-one counseling with Honey Bee advisors is part of her plan.

Because BIPOC community members are statistically more likely to be targeted by payday lenders and otherwise subject to financial difficulty, Honey Bee is also popular with employers' diversity, equity and inclusion teams. Ennie wants to be sure that all employees feel like they belong. Honey Bee now boasts that 89 percent of users are Black, Hispanic or Asian.

Focused on her social impact, Ennie has established Honey Bee as a Certified B Corporation. This designation demonstrates Ennie's commitment to prioritize mission over profitability even as she seeks both.

Ennie identified the problems in the marketplace after going through a divorce that hurt her credit rating and forced her to consider payday loans. She determined that there must be a better way. When she couldn't find one, she created one.

A critical element of Honey Bee's growth has been Ennie's effort to sell the program to employers. That has required her to connect with decision-makers in a way that leads to new clients. That's why she says connecting with people is her superpower. You can make it yours, too.

How to Develop Connecting With People as a Superpower

To connect with people in a way that they appreciate your personal experience requires you to evoke empathy. This is Ennie's superpower. You can make it yours by following the tips below.

1. *Ask questions.* To build a rapport with someone, you need to ask questions. Ennie is likely asking HR professionals questions about their employees. By asking qualitative queries, not just statistical ones, she can also learn more about the HR manager.
2. *Listen thoughtfully.* It is imperative to listen thoughtfully. You can't fake listening by just being quiet. You must focus on the message you hear and its implications. Demonstrate you are listening by asking relevant follow-ups.
3. *Show empathy.* Compassionately express a level of understanding for the challenges faced by the person you're connecting with. Ennie obviously demonstrates to HR professionals that she understands the problems they face trying to help employees in sticky financial situations.
4. *Be vulnerable.* This may be the most challenging part of connecting with people by evoking empathy. By courageously sharing something honest about yourself that could open you up to scorn, you trust your counterpart to feel and manifest compassion. Ennie has learned to do this by sharing the story of her divorce hurting her credit.
5. *Express gratitude.* When someone expresses sympathy or compassion, even if awkward or clumsy, you should express appreciation. Your gratitude is a sign of your strength, and it will help your counterpart feel rewarded for empathizing with you and your situation.

Ennie's success is due to the way she is vulnerable with people to establish a connection that leads to mutually beneficial action. You can follow her example and, with practice, make connecting with people your superpower.

Cheryl Dorsey

Chapter 5: Cultural Translation - Cheryl Dorsey

Devin: *Cheryl, what is your superpower?*

Cheryl: *So, I would say, and I tell young people this—and, Devin, I don't even think I figured this out until I was in my 40s, but I would say I am a cultural translator. I have the ability to move easily and diffuse across different spaces and navigate those pretty seamlessly. I'll often say I was an African-American kid who grew up in a predominantly Jewish neighborhood. Every year I celebrated Hanukkah as robustly as I did Christmas with my bubbe and zayde, who lived next door to me growing up. I played in my high school orchestra and spent the days playing Bach, Vivaldi, Beethoven, but couldn't wait to rush home and hear this newfangled music called rap that led to old school hip hop and felt equally comfortable with both traditions. I remember my early days of starting my Echoing Green project and being in the hallowed halls of Harvard Medical School during the day but walking across the subway tracks to some of the toughest neighborhoods in Boston. Both felt like home to me. And it's the same kind of cultural translation work I do today, talking about justice and equity in corridors of power that are more likely to be talking about bonds and private equity and hedge funds and being okay in all those spaces. So, I think that's probably my superpower.*

You can watch the full interview with Cheryl here: cheryl.s4g.biz.

Cheryl Dorsey might have become a literal rock star given her training in and love for music if she hadn't become a medical doctor, social entrepreneur and nonprofit leader, that is to say, a figurative rock star.

After finishing medical school at Harvard, with Nancy Oriol, she launched The Family Van, a nonprofit providing healthcare to the African American community in Boston. At the time, this population faced the third-highest infant mortality rate in the country.

In 1992, Cheryl received a fellowship from a young organization called Echoing Green. The included financial support was an essential part of bringing The Family Van to life. Nancy remains involved, and the program continues. When I visited with Cheryl, she reported that the organization had made about 108,000 visits, preventing illness for an estimated 5,648 people.

Cheryl joined Echoing Green about a decade after she received the fellowship. In the intervening years, she spent several years working in the Clinton Administration for the Department of Labor.

For nearly 20 years, she's led Echoing Green's efforts to identify and support promising changemakers. More than 800 people have now received fellowships. Its fellows launched Teach For America, City Year, One Acre Fund, SKS Microfinance and Public Allies, among many other high-impact organizations.

The organizations founded by Echoing Green fellows have touched the lives of millions of people across the country and around the world.

To accomplish all of this expansive social impact, Cheryl uses her superpower of cultural translation. It helps her find promising social entrepreneurs, raise money for the organization and otherwise communicate externally and internally.

How to Develop Cultural Translation as a Superpower

Cheryl notes that she initially developed her ability to communicate with disparate communities by growing up in a diverse neighborhood, where she observed both Christmas and Hanukkah. She certainly added to her capacity for cultural translation at Harvard, where she not only had a diverse group of friends, including the progeny of America's elite, she also had access to some of the rich and powerful themselves. After nearly a decade at Harvard, she had fully developed her superpower.

Few of us will have the opportunity to attend Harvard long enough to earn three degrees. Very few. But there are ways to develop this skill outside those walls.

First, the guiding principle for developing the ability to culturally translate among disparate groups is empathy, which is covered more specifically in Chapter 7. Start there. To form Cheryl's savant-level cultural translation skills, you also need to develop cultural fluency.

You learn cultural fluency primarily by immersing yourself in a culture. That is more difficult than it sounds. For a year, I lived in Guangzhou, China and yet didn't immerse myself truly in the culture. Without even a conversational ability to speak Mandarin, I learned a great deal but not nearly enough to become culturally fluent.

You can access the rich and powerful, if you'd like that cultural fluency, in various ways. Podcasting is one. Late last year, I was approached by a 15-year-old in Eastern Europe to be a guest on his podcast. I accepted. While I am certainly not among the rich and powerful, imagine the breadth of network this young man will build if he continues regular podcasts throughout high school. He could connect with over 100 international thought leaders, business leaders and politicians. It could provide the same sort of foundation that Cheryl created for herself.

Volunteering on political campaigns is another way to build a network that includes influential people. Not only do you get to meet the candidate, but you can also meet other volunteers and donors, including those you hope to meet.

Volunteering for nonprofits can lead to similar opportunities. Give enough time, and you'll get to know the staff. Then you may be invited to join an organizing committee. Perform well, and you could be invited to join the board. You will likely find some of the wealthy and powerful people you want to know among the board members.

Reading can accelerate your cultural fluency. Whether you want to know about the people of the Democratic Republic of the Congo or America's power elite, there are books, journals and blogs written every day that can help you accelerate your progress. Reading isn't a substitute for cultural immersion, but it speeds up the process of acculturation.

One note of caution: without becoming a group member—and some groups you can't join—you can never become a cultural native. You can become culturally fluent, enabling you to translate, much as you can become fluent in a language without ever achieving native-level language proficiency.

Given the years it takes, becoming the sort of cultural translator that Cheryl is may not be in the cards for you—at least not in the short run. If you want to improve your understanding of the people you hope to serve, the people who fund your work or the diverse set of people you work among, the above steps will allow you to add greater cultural fluency to your skillset. Remember to start with empathy.

Isabelle Hau

John Hewko, courtesy of Rotary International

Chapter 6: Diplomacy - Isabelle Hau and John Hewko

Isabelle Hau, Author

Devin: *Isabelle, what is your superpower?*

Isabelle: *My superpower: diplomacy.*

You can watch the full interview with Isabelle here: isabelle.s4g.biz.

John Hewko, Rotary International, CEO

Devin: *John, what is your superpower?*

John: *My superpower?*

Oh, I don't think I have superpowers. I do think, like any human being, I've got strengths and weaknesses. I do think I have an ability to sort of grasp a strategic vision and then sort of rally people around to try to achieve that and take people with disparate points of view and different perspectives and get them to kind of get to yes. And then move the ball forward, which is what makes this job so interesting because it is such a diverse, I mean—

Devin: *There are people in Rotary that have a different perspective?*

John: *You know, 1.2 million Rotarians, 1.4 million points of view. That's about as diverse as you can get. And I think that it's, on the one hand, a challenge, but for me, kind of an exciting thing. And I think one where I give, in my international experience, language skills. It's been kind of like trying to run the U.N., you know, on a much smaller scale. And I find it both interesting, intriguing and challenging.*

You can watch the full interview with John here: john.s4g.biz.

Isabelle Hau, an author with deep experience in the social sector, and John Hewko, CEO of Rotary International, both described their superpower as being diplomacy. Each has an extraordinary track record of impact that you should consider briefly before learning to be more diplomatic.

Starting with Isabelle, she helped lead Imaginable Futures, a philanthropic investment fund focused on education, as Omidyar Network spun it out. She had spent nearly a decade at ON responsible for leading impact investments in education. Previously, she had a successful career at Morgan Stanley, where I first met her. She earned an MBA at Harvard.

She is passionate about early childhood education because, in her birth country, France, she was cared for in subsidized childcare beginning at just three months of age and began attending no-cost pre-school at age 2 ½.

"Through these affordable and high-quality programs, I learned not [only] early literacy and early maths, but more importantly all the social-emotional learning skills that have helped [me] navigate my personal and professional journey," she explained.

She highlighted that children without adequate preparation upon enrolling in kindergarten are 25 percent less likely to graduate from high school and 60 percent more likely to skip college. Children who are not performing at grade level in the third grade have demonstrably more challenging lives.

At Imaginable Futures, she helped lead investments in education in the U.S. and abroad. Today, she is working on a book about the future of education.

As an investment banker and investor, she has been called upon to negotiate transactions even with a philanthropic purpose. In that role, she developed and used her superpower: diplomacy.

Similarly, John Hewko has used diplomacy as the top executive at Rotary International, which operates in more countries than the United Nations has members. Previously, as part of the Bush Administration, he was a senior official at the Millennial Challenge Corporation, working to support economic development in various African and other lower-income countries. Before that, he worked as an attorney in Eastern Europe.

At Rotary, the top priority is eradicating polio, an effort Rotary launched in 1985. John is passionate about the effort, personally helping raise over $50 million with an annual bike ride in Tucson, Arizona.

Rotarians play three primary roles fighting polio, John says. First, they raise money. The total raised by Rotary now tops $2 billion. Second, they advocate with governments around the world for financial support and cooperation with vaccination efforts. Third, Rotarians volunteer; hundreds of thousands have helped vaccinate children.

The impact has been dramatic, with the number of wild poliovirus cases dropping more than 99.9 percent from the 350,000 cases observed each year in the mid-1980s.

Significantly, diplomacy plays a vital role in the effort. Since the beginning, Rotary has partnered with the World Health Organization, U.S. Centers for Disease Control and UNICEF. The Gates Foundation joined the effort about two decades ago, and more recently, GAVI (the vaccine alliance) joined the partnership known as the Global Polio Eradication Initiative.

Diplomacy is a conscious part of the coordination effort among the GPEI partners. Not only are significant budgets determined, but lives hang in the balance. Negotiating with the best of intentions is essential.

Perhaps the most vivid example of diplomacy on the part of Rotary is working with warring parties to temporarily suspend fighting to allow for vaccinations—days of tranquility. For instance, Rotary has been successful in Sri Lanka and El Salvador. Sometimes, the pause in fighting has resulted in a long-term or permanent end to hostilities.

Rotary and Rotarians have also used diplomacy to respectfully combat vaccine resistance on a scale that varies from the most personal to multinational. The efforts have been successful, especially when people work in coordinated ways at every level, from neighborhoods up to the national leadership.

Diplomacy is a superpower that Isabelle and John have deployed in business, government and for social impact. You can, too.

How to Develop Diplomacy as a Superpower

Having read about how Isabelle and John use diplomacy for good, you are ready to learn more about being diplomatic.

John joined me for a follow-up conversation to discuss his insights. You can watch that second interview here: hewko.s4g.biz. He provided guidance on conducting negotiations diplomatically.

1. *Listen.* Effective diplomacy requires listening. By listening, you can understand and more thoroughly appreciate the other perspective. You can see how your different agendas align.
2. *Define agreements.* As you begin to negotiate, John suggests that you make an early effort to identify areas of agreement. Often, a document exists. It may be a contract, a joint public statement or a high-level mission and vision document. In any case, look for the points of agreement. Doing so serves two purposes. First, it builds confidence between the parties, and second, it accelerates the process so that the negotiation can proceed concerning points of disagreement.
3. *Narrow disagreements.* Once you identify the points of agreement, you don't have to work on them anymore. Move your attention to the topics in dispute. Work to define those points as narrowly as possible. Once that is done, both parties may agree that such tiny issues don't matter as part of the whole.
4. *Compromise.* If the points of disagreement do matter in the larger context, compromise is the final stage of diplomacy. Having built mutual confidence and a long list of points of agreement, you are in

a position to negotiate a compromise. You can work in good faith to resolve the final pain points.

By following John's guidance, you can develop your diplomatic skills. One day, diplomacy could become your superpower.

Leta Greene by Emily London

Chapter 7: Empathy - Leta Greene

Devin: *What is your superpower, Leta?*

Leta: *Well, my superpower—I've got to think about this because you've got to ask this question, and my first reaction was that I love people. But you know, in the case of this, I don't actually love all people, right? My superpower is that I see people, and I care about them, and I want the best for them. And that is why I've spoken out. It's because if I can help one boy or one girl realize that they can have a full and fulfilling and joyful, and amazing life, then it's worth sharing my vulnerable underbelly.*

You can view the full interview with Leta Greene here: leta.s4g.biz.

Leta Greene survived childhood sexual abuse but just barely. As a child, she blamed herself for what happened and, for a time, was suicidal over the experience. She overcame her experiences to lead a complete and happy life as an author, speaker and mother of three.

"I'm living joyfully, and I have fulfilling relationships with my husband, my children, and other people. The violation of being sexually molested from two-and-a-half to 14 years old—those are the fundamental years of who I am as a person—did not wreck me," she says. "I'm having a successful—in all ways—life."

In 2018, amidst an international discussion that came to be known as the Me Too movement, Leta wrote about her experience for the first time in her book, *Love, Me Too*. She hopes to help other people, men and women who are survivors of sexual abuse, recover as she has. She also wants to help prepare children better to understand how to avoid predators and inappropriate touching.

Now, she provides training on a range of topics, including maturation programs for 5th-grade girls, confidence workshops for tween and teen girls, seminars for parents on how to talk to your kids about sex, and she does keynote speeches on resiliency.

Leta is also supremely generous. Having known her for nearly a decade, I've observed her kindness in a variety of situations. The global pandemic brought out the best in her. She frequently organized food drives and worked to relieve people's suffering, including Native Americans, whose communities were hit especially hard by the virus.

Her childhood experience has helped her make empathy a superpower that enables her to be more effective as a professional speaker, in her volunteer and charitable work and as a mother.

How to Develop Empathy as a Superpower

Genes have been shown to influence one's ability to feel empathy for others. Still, research also demonstrates that intentional practice can help you increase your ability to put yourself in another's shoes.

Here are six tips psychologists use to help you develop your empathy.[3]

1. *Be curious.* To better put yourself in another's place, ask them about their lives and their experiences. Follow them on social media. Read what they have to say. This can be especially important for understanding members of other social, ethnic or religious groups.
2. *Be teachable.* To develop this aspect of empathy, you may need to step out of your comfort zone and find yourself attempting to do things you don't know how to do. Whether it is finding a restroom in a bustling city far from home, writing software for the first time or cooking an unfamiliar dish, learn to ask for help and guidance.

---

[3] Positive Psychology, "Developing Empathy: 8 Strategies & Worksheets for Becoming More Empathetic," Jeremy Sutton, PhD, December 10, 2020, https://positivepsychology.com/empathy-worksheets/.

3. *Listen better.* Learning to be a better listener may require you to ask others about your listening skills. Be prepared to implement suggested changes.

4. *Check your biases.* If you don't think you have biases, visit Harvard's implicit bias self-test at bias.s4g.biz. Most people find that the test reveals biases they didn't recognize. I sure did. With eyes open, you are in a better position to judge less and learn more about others.

5. *Help others.* To develop a better understanding of people in other communities and situations, join them in nonprofit work. Spending a morning planting trees with members of another community in their neighborhood can give you a taste of what it is to walk in their shoes. Join them in common cause for the long haul to get the full experience.

6. *Read widely.* Though your time is valuable, reading from a variety of perspectives, from newspapers to fiction, is shown to help develop greater capacity for empathy.

Much has been written about developing empathy. You don't have to experience something as terrible as Leta did to understand another's journey. Learning to put yourself in the place of a fellow human being is a powerful tool for anyone hoping to do more good.

Jonathan Foley

Chapter 8: Fence Traveling - Jonathan Foley

Devin: *Jonathan, what's your superpower?*

Jonathan: *I don't know. I know what my kryptonite is; I have a bunch of those. I guess one thing I like to do—I don't know how good I am—but I like to be kind of a fence traveler. I think that it's an uncomfortable place to sit—on the edge of a fence. It can become uncomfortable. You can fall off. But I like to have one foot in the world of the science and one foot in the world of the real world. And how do you take really good, rigorous science into the real world? But more importantly, how do you take the concerns of everyday folks, businesses, communities and so on back to the scientists? Say, hey, you're doing great work over here, but you're not asking the right questions. What people need to know is this. And so I guess that's why I like to do a little bit of shuttle diplomacy or fence-straddling, whatever you want to call it, between the scientific world and the real world. And it's just really important in both directions. So it's not just the science talking, informing people; it's not a megaphone.*

I remember my mom used to say something, too; it's pretty funny. We're born with two ears and one mouth; try to use them in that ratio. So, it's important to listen much more than we speak. And I think we'd all do a little better if we did that.

You can watch the full interview with Jonathan at jon.s4g.biz.

Jonathan Foley leads Project Drawdown, a nonprofit that is working to reverse climate change by lobbying for the implementation of existing technologies, practices and policies that will reduce not only the amount of carbon we emit but also the level of carbon in the atmosphere.

In 2017, Project Drawdown published the book *Drawdown: The Most Comprehensive Plan Ever Proposed to Reverse Global Warming,* edited by Paul Hawken (also featured in this book for his superpower).

The most remarkable thing about our conversation was Jonathan's optimism. With a clear sense of urgency, but without a hint of defeatism or despair, referring to reversing climate change, he pronounced, "This may be the single biggest business opportunity in human history."

He explained that we humans need to fundamentally reinvent society from the ground up to eliminate carbon. He sees this as an opportunity for businesses to prosper and for humans to thrive as we develop more equitable and inclusive models.

Given his remarkable optimism, it is interesting that he sees his capacity to travel along the fence between scientists and the rest of the world as his superpower. I suspect, however, that the optimism comes from the confidence he has developed about the future, given his work. By influencing the behavior of business leaders and scientists, he is influencing an acceleration of drawing down the carbon in the air. Of course, he is optimistic. He can not only see the future, but he can also bend it. That is some serious Man of Steel stuff.

How to Develop Fence Traveling as a Superpower

Jonathan works between the scientific community, where his career began, on the one hand, and on the other what he calls "the real world" where businesses and laypeople live their lives, barely aware of the work going on in science. Most people find themselves situated between or among two or more disparate groups, like Jonathan.

What are the disparate communities in your life? Your colleagues at work are likely to represent one. Perhaps the people your organization serves represent another (you may call them customers or clients). Nonprofits often have a third audience to address: donors, a hardly homogenous group. You can probably identify at least two groups you communicate with regularly. Learning to travel the fence between them could help you change the world. Consider the following steps to help you.

1. *Listen.* This skill comes up a lot in this section of other-oriented superpowers. It is critical here. You'll need to be able to hear and understand what both groups are telling you.
2. *Probe.* To understand and work with two or more disparate groups, you need to probe for what they're not saying. Ask questions to get below the surface.
3. *Analyze.* When you serve as an intermediary helping disparate groups better understand one other, analyze what both sides tell you.
4. *Find common ground.* It may be tempting to focus first on differences. But it will be more productive to find the groups' shared interests, language and goals before you shift to identifying the differences.
5. *Identify differences.* With years of experience, Jonathan was able to see the scientists weren't asking some of the questions that business leaders were. Look for differences in the situations, goals and objectives between your groups.
6. *Share.* Now that you can see what others may not, it is time to let them in on the secret. Help both groups learn about the differences in perspective and intent you observe to help them understand one another and work together more effectively.

As you contemplate this superpower and the steps required to master it, you may feel intimidated. Years of experience within two groups will give you more capacity to facilitate communication between them than hours, days or weeks. Still, using this approach from the moment you identify your role among separate communities will enable you to have more impact from the start.

Shelby Hintze

Chapter 9: Helping Others Feel Comfortable - Shelby Hintze

Devin: *Well, Shelby, what's your superpower?*

Shelby: *Oh geez, I would hope that my superpower would be making people feel comfortable and willing to open up. I try really hard to be vulnerable with people as well so that they feel that they can be that way with me. I create—it's a silly word—but a safe space for them. Helping people feel comfortable, have a little fun and maybe forget about troubles that they're having or a place that they can talk about those as well. I hope that's what it is. Well, I don't know if it is, but that's the goal, at least.*

You can watch the full interview with Shelby here: shelby.s4g.biz.

Shelby Hintze is a producer at NBC affiliate KSL in Salt Lake City, Utah. She helps determine who and what goes on her shows and is a leader with significant influence. She also has spinal muscular atrophy.

Her experiences have led her to raise her voice toward greater inclusion for members of disadvantaged communities in the organizations that serve them. To put a finer point on it, she notes that there are not enough leaders at the organization that supports and advocates for people with her condition who have her condition. Even parents have a different perspective from those who have the condition.

When Shelby moved to Provo, Utah, to attend Brigham Young University, she reached out to the organization for guidance on finding a personal aid and other tasks associated with living independently for the first time in her life. She was disappointed by the response and noted that the organization lacked sufficient input from people with her lived experience. "That was a really big blind spot that they had at that moment," she said.

Her lived experience has helped her develop empathy and awareness for what others are feeling and a desire to create a place for them to be comfortable expressing themselves. Her experience also allows her to be effective in her job as a television producer.

Just once, I had the opportunity to be a guest on one of the shows she produced. She met me in the lobby and guided me through the labyrinth, that is the maze of production studios, where shows are produced. She was just the sort of person she describes. Working to put me at ease, she helped me prepare thoughtfully to face the cameras.

How to Develop Helping Others Feel Comfortable as a Superpower

Psychologists note that our brains developed to identify threats, including social ones. As a result, when you do anything the least bit threatening, even if it is unintentional, others will immediately perceive it using the reptilian part of the brain that constantly scans for risks.[4]

The adage, "Give no one cause to fear you," is a good start to making people feel comfortable.

Here are six ways to help others feel more comfortable around you.

1. *Express warmth.* In the most natural and authentic way possible, start conversations with a compliment, praise or expression of interest. Even a kind remark about the context of the meeting—the room you're in, the weather, the subject of the meeting—will help.
2. *Be vulnerable.* As Shelby notes, she tries to be vulnerable to create a safe place for others where they can let down their guard.
3. *Remain calm.* The more excited you are, the more others may become nervous around you, fearing that something unpredictable could happen.

---

[4] Psychology Today, November 9, 2015, "What Puts People at Ease?" Rick Hanson, Ph.D., https://www.psychologytoday.com/us/blog/your-wise-brain/201511/what-puts-people-ease

4. *Exude chill.* Speak slowly to avoid rattling people with a barrage of words.
5. *Avoid anger.* Even if your anger is directed toward people who are not present (politicians in Washington, bankers on Wall Street, customer service agents at your cable company) you will immediately make others uncomfortable if you express it emotionally.
6. *Listen.* Just listening is vital for making others feel at ease around you. Giving them a chance to fully express themselves without being interrupted helps them feel respected.

While making others feel comfortable the way Shelby does may not be your superpower, these simple things can at least help you get through a networking event or cocktail hour without feeling like you've left a trail of awkward conversations.

Allie Barnes

Amit Bouri

Chapter 10: Listening - Allie Barnes and Amit Bouri

Allie Barnes, CEO of Village Capital

Devin: *Allie, what is your superpower?*

Allie: *Oh boy! I think it's listening. I have been more of a behind-the-scenes player. I started my career in communications. I was really about lifting other voices up and really spending time sharing the innovative and exciting things other people were doing. That forces you to be a good listener in order to be able to tell stories effectively. So I'd say that, you know, as a leader in an organization, you have to be able to effectively listen.*

You can watch the full interview with Allie here: allie.s4g.biz.

Amit Bouri, Founder and CEO of the Global Impact Investing Network

Devin: What is your superpower?

Amit: I don't know if I have a superpower, but I think in the business that I'm in, the thing that I'm most proud of is the time I spent listening and learning from others. We have a global network that, of course, we've talked a lot about the resources in terms of financial capital, but we didn't spend as much time talking about the talent and intellectual capital that we have in that group. And the reason why we started as a network and why I'm glad we're a network now, though a much bigger network, is that we are engaging the best thinkers from around the world—true pioneers working in countries all around the world. At our last conference in Paris, we had people from 80 countries. My expectations are high for the event they were holding in Amsterdam in October. But what my job is in many ways is being part of a kind of hub of this network, and that's what the GIIN's organization and our team do. I'm always listening, learning, trying to push my thinking, trying to engage others in how we can form a better network for collective action. That's the superpower that I try to hone as much as possible and hopefully is in plentiful use.

You can watch the full interview with Amit here: amit.s4g.biz.

Interestingly, Allie Barnes and Amit Bouri have the same superpower and work in the same industry, but I didn't speak to them together. They didn't compare notes for our separate discussions. Allie is the CEO of

Village Capital, a firm that makes impact investments in startups organized to solve social problems. Amit is the founder and CEO of the Global Impact Investing Network, almost always abbreviated as the GIIN, which is a formal network of people like Allie.

As she explained, Allie began her career in public relations, requiring her to listen and understand the messages of other people and organizations. Her success in that field brought her into the orbit of billionaires Jean and Steve Case. She worked at their venture fund, Revolution and later more closely still with Jean at the Case Foundation.

The Case Foundation partnered with Village Capital on the Rise of the Rest effort to enhance entrepreneurship and venture capital investing outside California, New York and Massachusetts. She joined Village Capital during that time, helping to execute the nationwide effort. So, when founder Ross Baird stepped down from his position as CEO to pursue new impact opportunities, she was tapped to replace him.

Allie is duly proud of the work she and Village Capital have done. Careful third-party analysis of its completed transactions demonstrates that it effectively reduces gender bias in startup investing. The Village Capital model uses a peer-selection model. The partners in the fund don't make investment decisions. They put the candidate investee entrepreneurs through an extensive accelerator training program; at the end, the participants choose the top two companies for investment.

Allie built her career from the ground up to use business to solve social problems. Now, she works in a niche that didn't even have a name when she was in college. Impact investing got its name in 2008 after she launched her career in corporate social responsibility. Her career path is proving to be both upward and impactful.

Amit Bouri founded the GIIN with a similar mission, to organize and expand the network of people making impact investments and find ways to support them. Few people can claim to have done more to advance the practice and increase the capital deployed in impact investing than he.

When I visited with him in June of 2019, he reported that global impact investments—narrowly defined—had reached $502 billion. The narrow definition is essential. There are wide ranges of estimates of total impact investments precisely because there is some disagreement about what experts should count.

"Impact investments are investments made into companies, organizations, and funds with the intention to generate social and environmental impact alongside a financial return," Amit says. "Impact investments can be made in both emerging and developed markets and target a range of returns from below market to market rate, depending upon investors' objectives."

This definition excludes what some now estimate to include trillions of dollars of capital managers screen for environmental, social, and corporate governance failures, a practice called ESG or socially responsible investing. While Amit celebrates this capital, he notes that the companies and investors don't have the same intentionality and often settle for the omission of negative impacts.

Amit was inspired to build the organization and grow impact investing because he recognized that traditional resources, governments and nonprofits, lacked sufficient financial resources to solve some modern problems, including climate change. By bringing profit-oriented capital into the mix, he accesses a new source to fight old challenges.

Amit's role and success in driving scale mean that he deserves credit for saving countless lives, helping millions lift themselves out of poverty and decelerating the out-of-control freight train that is global warming. How much credit he deserves is debatable, but I would certainly argue he deserves more than he gets.

As we look at these two investment professionals, their impressive careers and results—and their differences—it is curious to find them both rely on the same superpower: listening.

How to Develop Listening as a Superpower

You could describe me, having interviewed more than 1,200 people, as a professional listener. The one thing I can say with confidence on this topic is that I could be a better listener. You can be a better listener, too, even if you don't struggle with it the way I do.

Here are some pointers I've drawn from journalist and leadership expert Adam Bryant's expansive New York Times piece on listening.[5]

1. *Be present.* When you listen, you need to eliminate all distractions. Silence and hide your phone. Turn off your monitor. Focus your attention. This also requires that you stop thinking about your response to what you hear. It is natural to think about a conversation as a two-way street, but if your goal is to listen, learn and understand, you have to give up your agenda. You can gamify being present by thinking of it like improv. Force yourself to be ready at any instant to react to what others say like you're a member of an improv theater troupe.
2. *Don't judge.* Listening is a manifestation of empathy, so review and reflect on all you learn in Chapter 7. You can't listen effectively

---

[5] New York Times, Smarter Living, "How to Be a Better Listener," https://www.nytimes.com/guides/smarterliving/be-a-better-listener

and judge the speaker at the same time. Skip the judgment. Remember the acronym W.A.I.T., which stands for Why Am I talking? To be a good listener, you shouldn't be talking about yourself except to relate more effectively to the other person.

3. *Listen actively.* This vital concept says you should engage in the conversation to demonstrate that you are listening. For instance, use body language like nodding to replace crossing your arms across your chest. Listen carefully enough that you can periodically recap what the other person says to confirm your understanding.

4. *Learn.* Amit described his superpower as "listening and learning," which is a good goal for every conversation. Seek to learn something. Trying to learn will help you ask more thoughtful, open-ended questions to elicit greater insight. As you seek to learn from everyone, you'll become a better listener.

Listening is the sort of superpower that will make you better at just about anything. However you want to make a difference in this world, listening will help you do it better. It is a critical skill for demonstrating empathy and love. Becoming a better listener will help you become a better person.

Shaun Paul

Chapter 11: Listening and Bridging Vision to Action - Shaun Paul

Devin: *Shaun, what is your superpower?*

Shaun: *My superpower? I think about two things; a key one is listening. It's just so important to listen well. It's something that doesn't happen enough in the world. So who are my customers? Who are my stakeholders? What are their needs? What are their aspirations? How do I reconcile those needs and aspirations of my stakeholders— stakeholders being farmers, community leaders, investors, industry? So listening really well, I think with an empathetic ear, I think that would be one, "secret sauce."*

I think the other thing that helps me do what I do is being able to bridge an inspiring vision and turn it into an executable plan. I work in an environment where some people love to dream and brainstorm. A lot of other people— that makes them nervous and uncomfortable. Many people need clarity and certainty. So I'm a great bridge builder between envisioning the world of possibilities and building a bridge into what's actionable and doable—so bridging vision to action.

You can watch the full interview with Shaun here: shaun.s4g.biz.

Shaun Paul, CEO of Ejido Verde, is doing high-impact work on two fronts at once. By helping small-holder farmers in Michoacan, Mexico, to replant pine forests to harvest pine resin, he's leading an effort that serves both to save the planet and help people. Collectively, those farmers could see their businesses increase in value by over a billion dollars. The scale of environmental impact experts will measure should run parallel.

For about 90 years, people in this area of Mexico have harvested and sold pine resin. Though relatively unknown, the global market for it is at least $10 billion annually. Sadly, over three decades beginning in the 1980s, deforestation became a problem, and production has dwindled. Because those who cut the trees stole them, the community suffered even more acutely than the environment. Farmers lost assets and income.

Under Shaun's leadership, Ejido Verde has fostered a restoration of old business models layered with modern support. The company provides financing to the farmers to help them plant new trees and survive until the trees start producing resin after about ten years.

Ejido Verde helps the farmers design their farms for intercropping, including free-range animal grazing, which will provide the farmers with additional income.

Farmers are now cultivating 4,200 hectares of pine forest, about 70 percent of the area of Manhattan. Shaun's goal is to reach 12,000 hectares or about the equivalent of two Manhattans.

The contracts with farmers require them to keep the trees in production until 20 years after planting. At that point, the farmers' obligations to Ejido Verde are complete. Farmers then have the option to continue harvesting pine resin or harvest the trees. Shaun is encouraging farmers to keep the pine resin business going as a means of continuing to sequester more carbon.

Shaun's work is changing the world at a stunning scale and serving the needs of both the community and the planet.

How to Develop Listening and Bridging Vision to Action as Superpowers

Shaun's paired superpowers are different on the surface, but as I explored them with him, I began to see the harmony between them. Listening and bridging vision to action are two separate—but I think you'll agree—related skills.

You can watch our second interview focused on his superpowers here: shaun2.s4g.biz.

In the last chapter, you learned powerful insights about listening. In this chapter, you will read suggestions that may overlap a bit but come directly from Shaun's experience.

He introduced this topic with a quick anecdote about his Latina wife. It took a decade of marriage to learn that when he asked her if she was hungry and she responded, "a little," she meant a lot. Listening is a skill he continues to develop.

Let's dive into the topic of listening. Here are the three essential principles that guide Shaun to be an effective listener.

1. *Empathy.* To listen with empathy means that you assign no blame. You leave your ego out of the conversation entirely. No judgment is allowed. To hear what others are saying, you must put aside the filters and noisemakers in your head. Listening is about focusing on the other person.
2. *Ask questions.* One guidepost is to ask a lot of questions. Shaun sees that people aren't always eager to share their concerns, but you need to hear them. He encourages everyone to ask clarifying questions. Don't fall into the temptation to be argumentative. Finally, focus on the elephant in the room. Too often, people talk around the big issues rather than about them. Go there.
3. *Find perspective.* To get the view you need, talk to lots of people. Hear many voices. Don't let the conversation with one or two color your understanding of an entire population.

By applying these lessons, you can undoubtedly become a better listener. Imagine what you can accomplish if listening becomes your superpower.

Shaun's second superpower is bridging vision to action. He notes that he often deals with people, including some of the investors in Ejido Verde, who see the big picture and the mission. At the same time, he deals with accountants, engineers, chemists and the like, who are focused more on the tasks at hand. Helping the two groups work together is a key to his success.

Here are the three guiding principles for bridging vision to action from my conversation with Shaun.

1. *Set goals.* Both the visionaries and the task-oriented members of the team can see value in specific, measurable goals. Build them across time frames, including as little as 30 days, so the less visionary can focus on action.
2. *Discuss failure.* To bridge this divide, Shaun says, you need to hold people—including yourself—accountable for failures and forgive them. You need to model the behavior. Stand up, when appropriate,

to say, "I failed" or "I made a mistake." People need to know that when doing challenging things, you pair accountability with forgiveness. Note, however, that doesn't mean tolerating negligence.

3. *Focus on results.* Perhaps the most critical principle for bridging the visionary and the action-oriented is focusing on and reporting results. Create a dashboard of data. Show the numbers and the details. Note the progress made toward longer-term goals. The big-picture-people will love to see the results just as much as the doers will take pride in them.

By following these principles, you can better connect the people who are thinking about your work differently. Getting them on the same page will help you drive more results and keep everyone moving in the same direction. Even if you don't choose to make this your superpower, remember to employ these principles whenever you can. Imagine the difference it will make in your impact.

Emily Wright

Chapter 12: Love - Emily Wright

Devin: Emily, what is your superpower?

Emily: My superpower? Probably my heart. I just love people. And for me, too, whether it's Haiti, or Somalia, or Kenya, or whether I'm in Taiwan speaking in front of thousands of people, it doesn't matter if I can connect with people's hearts. To me that's my greatest strength is for them to know how much I love them and how much love they are deserving of.

The following is how I described my discussion with Emily for Forbes in an article called "Global Impact Comes From Female Cofounder's Success With $1B Enterprise." You can watch the full interview here: emily.s4g.biz.

"The reason I get up in the morning is to be able to truly give back to humanity. I think we've been given a responsibility to do that," says Emily Wright, co-founder of dōTERRA, the private manufacturer and distributor of essential oils.

The scale of the business gives her an unusual ability to have an impact. She notes that the company generates a profit on more than $1 billion in annual revenue. Her current title is founding executive, sales and marketing.

Working with a founding team of six men, she says of women, "I think we think a bit differently." Of working with an all-male team, she adds, "I love the way they think and everything they contribute; I think they appreciate what I contribute."

It wasn't always like that. In a previous company, Wright says she sat on a board of four, working her way up from executive assistant to become an executive herself. "I had to work a lot harder in order to achieve that position," she says, adding, "I was paid about half the amount of the men."

Because of challenges she faced early in her career, Wright says, "What I love most is empowering other women."

"I know what it feels like to be in their shoes," she says of other women. "I know what it feels like to have $26 in my checking account, wondering how in the world I'm going to put food on the table for my children. I know what it feels like to go hungry. I know what it feels like to lose my identity. I know what it feels like to get beaten up and tossed aside by the world."

DōTERRA reports having 2,000 employees and 3 million "Wellness Advocates" who buy the products and sell them to their friends in a network marketing program. Most of the Wellness Advocates are women, giving Wright influence with millions of them.

Since the founding of the company, Wright has had responsibility for sourcing raw materials and the company's social responsibility initiatives. She has helped to infuse sourcing with a sense of mission and purpose. Even before the company became profitable, she says the founders agreed to "create a culture of giving back." The founders personally funded the creation of the Healing Hands Foundation, a 501(c)(3) nonprofit.

She recalled a sourcing visit to Haiti in 2013. During the visit with local suppliers, she was taken aback by a gentleman who got up and said through a translator, "I have a dream to someday have clean water." She learned that the community had to travel three hours each day to retrieve water that then had to be boiled to be safe to drink.

Since then, Wright reports that dōTERRA has not only provided clean water by drilling wells in the community but has also constructed schools, clinics and community centers as well as providing them with sustainable income via the purchase of essential oils.

One of the most challenging environments for sourcing raw materials is Somalia, dōTERRA's primary source of frankincense.

Wright recalled her first visit to the country. Upon her arrival with CEO David Sterling, she saw a complete lack of hope in the people's faces. "We have to change this." She says they immediately agreed.

It has taken time, but the company has invested in the community that grows frankincense, providing warehouses with running water and sanitation for processing and schools for both their boys and girls. They have also built a clinic and have begun work on a hospital.

Wright boasts that the income of the frankincense growers has increased fivefold as dōTERRA worked to eliminate intermediaries who leveraged the desperate situation of the growers to buy from them at abusive prices.

Similarly, dōTERRA established sourcing operations in Bulgaria in 2015. Stoyana Stoeva, co-founder and partner in the local social enterprise called the Social Tea House, said that dōTERRA had been a partner since its founding in 2016.

The Utah-based company paid to reconstruct a three-story building that hosts a "tea saloon," seminar space and coworking space. With help from dōTERRA, the Social Tea House has created a line of locally sourced merchandise that helps fund its social mission.

Stoeva credits dōTERRA with helping accomplish its goals: to mentor young people with limited opportunities by providing them with skills, from non-violent communication to responsibility and financial management.

Wright remains optimistic. She describes the Somalia project as "probably" the most challenging project they've completed. "What's next?" she asks eagerly.

Despite all of this, she says, "What I want to be known most as is the world's greatest mom."

How to Develop Love as a Superpower

Emily has learned to use love as a language to allow her to communicate with other people, especially women, who may at first glance appear to have little in common with her. Not only has this connection helped the women she seeks to serve through her work—including both the women who supply essential oils and those who sell them—but it has also helped her play a leadership role in growing a billion-dollar-plus business.

Can you imagine how love could help you do more good? The following three steps will help you feel, express and reflect a love for the people you work with and serve.

1. *Recognize their worthiness.* You have chosen your colleagues, employees and the people you serve. One way or another, they have been screened and found worthy. Own that decision. Choose now to love them. Consider the value of the relationships and how much each individual in the group means to you. You should see their intrinsic worth as human beings, not just as colleagues and subjects of your philanthropy.

2. *Express your love.* Nothing will help you feel love for others more than saying it. This is likely for two reasons. First, your sense of integrity will require that you speak the truth, so when you say it, you will feel it. Second, those to whom you express your love will reflect it, making it mutual.

3. *Model love.* If you don't behave consistently with your words, you will find your message not just ignored but also rejected, and you will harm the relationship you want to build. So, treat your employees, colleagues and those you serve with respect—the way you want them to treat you.

It is appropriate to tell a room full of people, including employees or people you serve, that you love them. On the other hand, it is inappropriate in many one-on-one situations to say, "I love you."

Love can become your superpower for good.

Brian Vo by Willis Bretz Photography

Chapter 13: Translating English to English - Brian Vo

Devin: Brian, before we go, what is your superpower?

Brian: It's a humbling question.

I think it would be translating English to English. Think of being able to hear what the health person is saying and knowing what is most important and relevant for the finance person and vice versa. And then throw government and the public sector into that mix. I think that's been one of the most enjoyable—hair-pulling but enjoyable—and most impactful breakthroughs I've been a part of.

You can watch the full interview with Brian here: brian.s4g.biz.

Brian Vo is not your typical Wharton MBA. He specializes in international development finance aimed at ending poverty and improving public health.

We spoke during Brian's tenure with Pact Ventures, a venture program launched by the nonprofit Pact. In that capacity, he was developing a variety of financing structures, custom fit to the circumstances. In the spring of 2021, Brian took a new position doing similar work for the international development finance company DAI.

He noted that grant capital could be considered the most risk-tolerant capital. Unlike venture capital, which is often seen as quite risk-tolerant but expects to not only get its money back but with great returns, nonprofit grants expect no financial return. Economic interventions proven to yield results that shouldn't be considered risky are still being funded by donations. They can repay part or all of the funding. His work was designing funding strategies custom fit to the projects.

In this work, he saw he was adept at solving one barrier to progress. English speakers from different functional areas had difficulty explaining their needs and objectives to one another. "English is not English is not English," he says.

As he joined in discussions with each group, he learned how they talk about each other and how they frame the same problem differently. Jargon, he notes, has different meanings in one group than in another, so they are saying the same thing but meaning something different. At other times, he found, the disparate groups would say different words but intend the same meaning.

For example, he notes that his colleagues in finance would focus on numbers, statistics and repayments. In contrast, his colleagues on the health side, the folks with master's degrees in health, would focus on what works and what doesn't for treating and preventing AIDS.

One particular sticking point, he found, is the implication that a financial value could be or should be assigned to human lives.

By helping the disparate groups communicate more effectively, he was able to accelerate impact. Brian would be the first to say he shouldn't get credit for all of Pact's work, but consider some of these statistics. Over 2 million people received improved access to healthcare, 1.4 million increased their income or savings, 2.3 million got help improving natural resource management and helped 67,000 people get better access to energy. If his talent for translating English to English only moved these numbers a bit, he helped countless individuals.

How to Develop Translating English to English as a Superpower

You are likely to remember when you were in a situation straddling two different groups with somewhat different perspectives. Perhaps you can recall planning a family event where you discovered that your in-laws had a different expectation than you for some of the details. Reflect on a situation when you had to explain your department's work to someone in another department. Do you remember feeling some stress?

You can learn to be an effective information broker like Brian. Here are some ideas to help you develop this skill.

The first step is to listen. Steven Covey famously noted that highly effective people seek first to understand and only then to be understood. In Chapter 10, you learned more from some superheroes in this book who use listening as a superpower and how you can, too.

The following three tactics will help you become a better English-to-English translator.

1. *Earn trust.* You can earn the trust and respect of the groups you hope to help understand one another by respecting group values and individual group members. You'll also gain confidence on all sides by being trustworthy. Show up when scheduled. Report honestly and accurately on meetings and results. Give credit where due.
2. *Invest time.* By being in the room with each participating group, you will learn and earn. You'll learn more about the context for their positions, opinions and values, and you'll earn credibility and respect.
3. *Learn jargon.* Learning technical jargon is tough enough, but watching for nuanced differences in meaning is a particular challenge. Brian saw that financial folks and health professionals sometimes used the same words to mean different things. I imagine that when a financial professional refers to "return on investment," for instance, they mean something different from someone on the health side using that jargon. The finance person is more likely referring to a purely financial calculation, while the public health expert may be thinking of lives saved.

Your organization needs more help in this area. Even if you have a perfect culture internally, your external partners are not likely thinking about English-to-English translation as a problem. They are not likely thinking about how their distrust or skepticism about your organization's intentions may muddle communication.

As a result of this need, if you can master this skill by conscientiously following the above steps (don't forget to listen), you will become more valuable to your organization and the world. You will make a more significant impact and do more good.

Davinia James-Stewart by Lyndon George

Chapter 14: Unconditional Love - Davinia James-Stewart

Devin: Speaking of power, what is your superpower?

Davinia: My superpower is that I have the capacity to accept love and just give it right back to the world. I think that love is the foundation behind everything that I do. It is a source that I feel that can never end. I am filled with it. I receive it, and I openly give it without wanting anything in return.

You can watch the full interview with Davinia here: davinia.s4g.biz.

Davinia James-Stewart was born in Jamaica to a teenage mother with few resources, financial or otherwise. She was taken in and raised by another woman, an activist, who provided all her basic needs and helped her succeed in school. At age 11, this woman who had cared for her all these years passed away, and Davinia went to live with her biological mother, experiencing the twin perils of poverty and violence for the first time.

Shortly after moving in with her mother, Davinia faced an extraordinary experience returning home from school with her brother. Held at gunpoint by a local thug, her brother yelled for his sister to run.

Frozen by fear, she didn't move even as the thug held his gun to her brother's chest.

"Run," he screamed. And she did.

Frantic, she shrieked as she entered her home, "He's dead! He's dead!" Her mother "went into superwoman mode."

Together they ran back to find her brother still with the barrel of a gun in his chest. Their mother pulled the gun to her own chest and said, "If you want him, you're going to have to go through me."

The gunman, ashamed or afraid of the consequences of killing a woman, walked away.

As an adult having immigrated to the U.S., Davinia realized that girls around the developing world face the sort of challenges she did in Jamaica. She decided to do something about it and organized a nonprofit she calls Pennies4Girls.

To date, she has raised 2.5 million pennies and paid for 500 girls to attend school in Haiti, Cambodia, Nepal, Peru, Afghanistan, Egypt, Ethiopia, Sierre Leone, India and Nigeria. In addition, she and the organization have provided girls with reusable feminine hygiene to help them stay in school, avoiding missed days due to menstruation.

How to Develop Unconditional Love as a Superpower

Unconditional love can be your superpower, too. While we often think of love as a reciprocal emotion, especially in romantic love, the unconditional variety is unilateral. It represents a choice on your part to love others regardless of how they treat you.

That doesn't mean you have to put up with being mistreated; you can still manage a relationship in a healthy way, which may include discontinuing it. It *does* mean forgiving the hurt and the pain that others may cause you by their behavior.

Ultimately, unconditional love is about recognizing that humans are all worthy of love and respect. Virtually everyone feels love toward their mothers, their friends and family members. The challenge is to develop a love for people who do not seem to deserve it and certainly have not earned it with their actions toward you. Think of your political adversaries, criminals in your community and simple strangers.

Here are three tips you can use to develop your unconditional love:

1. *Forgive yourself.* This sounds easier than it is. Before you can forgive yourself, you need to identify and reflect on your mistakes—not so easy. Once you acknowledge your errors and then forgive yourself for making them, you give yourself permission to see the poor choices in others and forgive them, too. Forgiving others for their mistakes is a central part of unconditional love.
2. *Act as if.* It is more difficult to feel love for strangers or those you may see as opponents, but you can act as if you loved them. Ask

yourself, how would I behave toward this person if I truly loved them? Whether or not you can feel that love, you can act as if you do. Psychologists are pretty confident that changing our behavior changes how we feel. Smiling when we're not happy makes us feel more content. Acting out love will help you feel love.

3. *Practice daily.* Make a point to do something every day that demonstrates love toward a stranger or even an opponent. If you find yourself near the end of the day and haven't done it, think of someone across the political divide, a player for the other team, or just a stranger chosen at random, and send them a tweet, text or email with short but genuine praise. You can do it in just a moment; it will put your new skills to work and help you feel the power of unconditional love.

Even if you can't make this your defining characteristic, you can probably imagine how we all benefit from deploying a bit more unconditional love toward one another.

Part 2: Unique Superpowers

About a third of the superpowers people reported didn't align well with any of the groupings I defined for the book. Each was unique. Running the gamut from authenticity to uniqueness, these superpowers have equal potential to inform, empower and inspire you.

Steve Klass

Chapter 15: Agenda Merging - Steve Klass

Devin: Steve, what is your superpower?

Steve: My superpower is a form of problem-solving ideation; I call it agenda merging. This came out when I was a paid employee of state government or I was a private consultant. Frequently, you're called upon to help somebody, usually, a client or customer, to get past some barrier that they're really baffled by. And what I found is if you would just get over the fear and just walk up to that wall—think of barriers as a wall— you walk up close to the wall, what you find is, oh, there's a way to get over this wall. There's a way around this wall. There's a way we can pull down a couple of bricks in this wall. If we examine it closely, we find out there are stakeholders to us that care about what we care about that actually operate doors in this wall. And if we knock the right way and talk the right way and consider their agendas important, they'll open the door. Sometimes they'll help us tear down the wall. And so, that's my superpower: finding how to get around barriers by better engaging stakeholders, getting over fear and addressing barriers. Now, the limit to my superpower is it works on other people, but I can't make myself a billionaire or get my P3 toolkit in everybody's hands. I have barriers that I can't face. I need people outside of me to see my barriers. It's like you can't be a mirror for yourself. And so I think that's all great consultants have ever been is great mirrors for their clients one way or the other.

You can watch the full interview with Steve here: steve.s4g.biz.

Steve Klass founded the nonprofit P3 Utah in 2012 to help businesses adopt triple-bottom-line approaches to doing business. He sees the potential for corporations and small companies to drive solutions to social problems. While a typical enterprise would focus on profit only on the bottom line, P3 Utah helps companies add people and planet to the mix.

Steve created a sustainability matrix to guide businesses in developing their triple bottom lines.

P3 Utah Business Sustainability Matrix

	INWARD IMPACT	OUTWARD IMPACT
PEOPLE	**WORKPLACE** How can I improve well-being in my workplace?	**COMMUNITY** How can my workplace improve quality of life locally and globally?
PLANET	**RESOURCES** How can my workplace become more eco-friendly?	**ECOLOGY** How can my workplace preserve the planet?
PROFIT	**PRODUCTION** How can my workplace ensure quality & efficiency in what we produce?	**MARKETPLACE** How can my workplace lead in its industry?

Permission to use this information is granted when accompanied by attribution to P3 Utah © 2019

This inward and outward approach to developing a triple-bottom-line philosophy within a business is helpful. Steve is proud of this tool.

One feature of sustainable business that some people don't recognize is that some actions both improve sustainability and profitability. For instance, by reducing waste or energy consumption, a company can reduce its carbon footprint and improve profits.

Steve highlights the work of U.S. Synthetic, a company that manufactures diamonds. Employees are empowered to take actions that will improve productivity and reduce waste and energy consumption without approval from managers. By creating this autonomy, teams generate more efficiencies and find greater satisfaction in their jobs.

Another identified an opportunity to reduce healthcare costs by self-insuring and investing savings in preventive programs that have yielded cost savings and better health outcomes for employees and their families.

Steve has also worked to drive policy change on Utah's Capitol Hill, advocating for legal structures that better allow businesses to reprioritize outcomes to avoid legal pressures always to put financial profits first. Utah is now the only state in the U.S. with legal charters for benefit corporations, benefit limited liability companies and low-profit limited liability companies.

Steve describes the superpower that enables his work as agenda merging. You may want to think of it as practical empathy. He helps people find solutions by identifying the people who can remove barriers and then identifying common interests.

How to Develop Agenda Merging as a Superpower

You can develop Steve's ability for agenda merging, too. Follow these simple steps to help you solve problems, especially for others, by bringing a fresh perspective.

1. *Identify a barrier.* Using Steve's approach, an excellent place to start is to look for the obstacles that may exist that make solutions more difficult. Laws, money, policies, distances, tolls—in almost every problem situation, you can spot one or more things that either cause the challenge or prevent the solution.
2. *Find key people.* As you see the wall you want to open, look for people who have keys to the hidden doors. Often, they are people who make policies and decisions. It could be corporate leaders, government officials from local to national levels or individuals with ownership. Be sure to consider all the options. There may be several different people or groups with the ability to open various doors in the wall.
3. *See common ground.* Once you have a list of people and organizations, look for those with shared interests with the people you want to help. Their goals don't have to align perfectly, from top to bottom. You only need to find the intersection of their interests that will motivate someone to open the door.
4. *Create alignment.* Once you see the common ground, the final step is to help the parties align their interests at the doorway. Sometimes this will require that your clients make an acceptable adjustment. Frequently, you will need to explain to the key person how their interests align. Typically, an open conversation between parties can yield progress.

Agenda merging is a tactical approach to solving problems that is more effective when you apply other superpowers discussed in this book, including love, empathy and passion. Those skills may be harder to learn. Everyone can use Steve's superpower.

Paul Hawken

Chapter 16: Authenticity - Paul Hawken

Devin: *What is your superpower?*

Paul: *I've never used that term. I've never thought about it. I knew you were going to ask me that question, so I did think about it for that reason. I feel like everybody has a superpower. But it is there already; it's not, you know, aggregated or gained or bought or something you seek. It's there, innate in each person. It's revealed when you are able to sort of peel away the beliefs and delusions of the world that try to tell you who you are, what you should think and what is true and what is not true. And to the degree to which you can come into your native self, your native DNA–you know, of who Devin is–there's your superpower because you see clearly. You accept. You're at peace with yourself. You understand your thoughts are just your thoughts, and they're not real as opposed to being reality. And it is another way to fall in love with the world and be in gratitude for actually just being alive.*

You can watch the full interview with Paul here: paul.s4g.biz.

Paul Hawken was a challenging interview to get. He was the author of the book *Drawdown* and founder of the organization, Project Drawdown, that continues related research aimed at reversing climate change. The book has become one of the bestselling books in history on the environment.

Paul's approach and his attitude are fascinating. He started by exploring the best available plans for addressing the climate crisis and found that the best thinking didn't provide a clear path to hitting reasonable targets, like limiting global warming to 1.5 to 2 degrees. The plans, he said, relied too much on multinational corporations changing longstanding patterns at the cost of their profits or even existence.

He started from the ground up, aggregating the analysis of climate and other scientists to establish reasonable projections for how humans could limit carbon emissions or sequester more carbon. The key he used was to look for existing technologies that can scale.

The analysis yielded 100 interventions the team described in the book, 80 of which are already working, and the rest have great promise. This clear and promising path for climate change solutions was revolutionary and has fundamentally changed the discussion about reversing global warming.

Paul talks about two principles that guided his approach to the book.

First, he insisted on eliminating any bias. The book could only include facts as defined by the scientists. Avoiding any bias led to the inclusion of controversial climate remedies like nuclear power.

Second, he felt it was important not to assign blame. By focusing on outcomes from implementing solutions, he and the team avoided blame or shame.

The results go far beyond the publication of the book. Today, Paul's legacy continues under the leadership of Jonathan Foley, whom I profile in Chapter 8. The organization Paul created now updates the list and publishes it on the website drawdown.org.

Many climate activists deserve credit for bringing the climate crisis to the top of the public agenda, but few deserve more recognition for making the path for business and industry so compelling. If we act quickly to reverse global warming early, it will be in no small part due to Paul's contribution.

His superpower, authenticity, is unique. He makes a compelling case, however, that truly knowing yourself and aligning your behavior with what you know brings both peace and power.

How to Develop Authenticity as a Superpower

Paul argues that your authentic self is an innate superpower. The challenge, he implicitly acknowledges, is that you must learn to know yourself. He recommends that you "peel away the beliefs and delusions of the world that try to tell you who you are, what you should think and what is true and what is not true."

To learn how to "peel away" all of that and perform a deeper introspection than usual, I look to psychologists for guidance.[6] This six-point process will help you find yourself. Along the way, you may find more superpowers!

1. *Identify your values.* You will face a bit of a challenge throughout this process. To be successful, you must be honest about your values. One way to approach this is to think about choices you might have to make. Which cause or nonprofit deserves your money? Which should receive your time? Which people in your life do you primarily want to spend time with? Your spouse? Your friends? Parents? Use these choices to help you see what you value most.

2. *Note your interests.* What do you enjoy? What captures your attention? What do you watch most on Netflix? Beach or mountains? Classic literature or the latest John Grisham? What are the sorts of questions you ask Alexa? What topics prompt you to pay attention? Make notes about this over the next week.

3. *Be honest about your temperament.* Think about what upsets you and what calms you and brings peace. Do you feel better after quiet time alone or do you need to be with people? Some people like everything planned and executed accordingly; others like to go with the flow, living spontaneously.

4. *Find your biorhythms.* You need to know when you're at your best. While I think many of the world's great people are or were morning people, I'm certainly not. I'm at the top of my game in the afternoon and evening. I don't know which I hate more, going to bed or getting out of it. Think of when you're at your best. When you know, you can choose to do your most important work when you're at the top of your game.

5. *Choose a mission.* Some people feel like fate, destiny or the divine chose their mission for them. Most often, I see this when the mission aligns perfectly with their values, interests and temperament. Think about the mission you want for yourself, for those closest to you and for the world. The better the fit, the more your sense of purpose will motivate your action, helping you overcome the most challenging things you'll face.

---

[6]Meg Selig, Psychology Today, March 9, 2016, "Know Yourself? 6 Specific Ways to Know Who You Are," https://www.psychologytoday.com/us/blog/changepower/201603/know-yourself-6-specific-ways-know-who-you-are.

6. *See your superpowers.* Knowing yourself would be grossly incomplete if you failed to identify your strengths and skills. Rather than focus on the things you do better than other people do, think about the things you do better than other tasks you do. There is a parallel. You may want to make note of your weaknesses. Many leadership experts have concluded, however, that it is more effective to strengthen your strengths than overcome weaknesses. As you read this book, think about which superpowers represent your strengths and then focus on reinforcing them.

With this dedicated focus on authenticity, you can reach your full potential, exemplifying your superpowers and applying them for maximum effect in support of your values-aligned mission. Nothing can stop you!

Roberto Milk

Chapter 17: Balance - Roberto Milk

Devin: *So, Roberto, what is your superpower?*

Roberto: *Superpower? I think that the first thing that comes to mind is being a dad because I've got four kids. I somehow manage to balance it all, and I hope that they would think that I'm a great dad because I strive to be. So, I think that my superpower may be balance. It's something that I'm always working on, but something that I really strive to do better and better. And it's just really finding that balance so that I can be a great husband, a great father and also great at the business and what we do. That's the secret, I think, to life. It's really about balance and fitting it all in. It's feeling the gratitude and the appreciation for what you're doing so that you don't end up all stressed and full of anxiety, which could happen easily when you're so spread thin all over the place.*

You can watch the full interview with Roberto here: roberto.s4g.biz.

Roberto Milk has accomplished something I thought was impossible. It looks easy, but I promise it is not. Many people travel to low-income countries, purchase some beautiful and affordable pieces from local artisans, and think, "I'll sell these at home to help the artisan make a living." It almost never works.

There are so many challenges to selling goods in the United States that it is almost impossible to scale a business with a mission to help people far away. Usually, the challenges overwhelm the aspiring entrepreneur, and the project dies. Sometimes good people achieve modest scale serving a single, small community.

Roberto accomplished something out of this world. He founded Novica, which now reports having remitted $112 million to artisans around the world. That's some scale!

The reason this business model is so tricky is that the mission puts the focus on the artisan. Of course, successful salespeople argue that the focus should be on the customer. Roberto found success in the middle with a focus on quality. Novica accepts only about a third of the artists who apply. Those who the company takes receive coaching and mentoring to help them improve their quality.

Ultimately, a vital part of the success is that the artists put their names on the quality finished product, helping to build relationships that lead to repeat sales. In essence, Roberto found the balance between customer focus and artisan focus that allowed the mission-driven business to prosper.

Another factor, admittedly, was the relationship he built with National Geographic. Initially, Novica supplied products to the big brand's online store. Over time, Novica took over the operation. Today, National Geographic owns 19 percent of Novica.

Roberto's balanced approach to business may have grown out of his balanced approach to life. After all, he says it's his superpower. But he wasn't talking about how his balance led to successful business outcomes; he was talking about being a good husband and father.

How to Develop Balance as a Superpower

Millennials seem to have learned more about balance than prior generations, which often seemed to struggle with it. By learning how to enhance balance in your life like Roberto, you can do what he's done, simultaneously building a successful mission-oriented business even as he partners with his wife to raise four children.

Most people who struggle with work-life balance feel they spend too little quality time away from work. You can likely relate. However, you may be thinking that because your job is purpose-driven, you can't seek balance. You can. To be at the top of your game at work, you should. Here are seven tips to help you do better.

1. *Remember, nobody's perfect.* Even if you could define a perfect work-life balance, you couldn't achieve it. Don't make *perfect* the goal. Focus on creating a *better* balance.

2. *Start small.* You may feel like you need to make a massive change in your life. That may not be possible and could lead to more significant disappointment. Look for incremental changes you can make this week or this month and once you've done them, find more. Try the adage, under-promise and over-deliver.

3. *Disconnect.* Today, especially since more people work from home, devices connect us to the office, colleagues and clients every waking hour of the day—and some of our sleeping hours as well. You know what your boss expects and what they require. Look for opportunities to wedge some disconnected time into that small gap between expectations and requirements. See if you can't find some quiet time for yourself and your loved ones.

4. *Set limits.* Every situation is different, and you know best. Do you sometimes stay at work or on task just because nothing urgent demands your time at home? Look for ways to set reasonable limits on your time. You may also want to look for opportunities to improve your productivity during that time to see if you can't get all the work done in less time. If you can't get it all done, look to prioritize so you can always get the essential tasks done and still leave personal time.

5. *Exercise.* Research shows the most dramatic impact of physical activity is between spending zero minutes and twenty minutes each week doing it. Most people benefit from adding a bit more to their routine. Remarkably, it helps you relax and reduce stress. Remember to start small and find incremental progress periodically until you've found your sweet spot.

6. *Care for yourself.* You can't do your best work if you're not well. Take time to get checked out and follow the advice of your doctor. It takes no more time to eat a healthy diet than a poor one. Make small changes to your lifestyle that will improve your health and extend your life. The healthier you are, the more productive you can be.

7. *Vacation.* You need to take a break once in a while. Not only do you need a few minutes off every day to clear your head, but you also need a few days off every quarter or so to get perspective. Be sure not to take a vacation you can't afford; the financial stress will offset the relaxation. Take plenty of time with those who will travel with you to plan the trip. Much of the benefit of vacation is the anticipation. Take lots of photos, too, so you can enjoy reliving the highlights. Get the most out of every little holiday.

As you think about making balance your superpower, remember that your goal is not only to make your personal and family time a higher priority, but it is also to make you more productive at changing the world. As Stephen Covey would say, think win-win. Do more good at home and work.

Deborah Frieze

Chapter 18: Biomimicry - Deborah Frieze

Devin: *Deborah, what is your superpower?*

Deborah: *This is a little odd. So, and again this comes from my incredible learning from Margaret Wheatley. It's biomimicry. Let me explain. Biomimicry is the practice of solving problems by asking the question what would nature do. I actually use nature to think about a model for structuring what we do. In impact investing, there's this big argument about whether you get market-rate returns or it's concessionary. So this is interesting; if the market has given us inequality, why would I be referring to that when I'm designing my impact investing approach? So concessionary means the market but not that. And so I was like, how do we find a different teacher, a different model upon which to base our assessments of risk and return and liquidity and storage and accumulation?*

I'll give you an example of what I mean. So when I'm stuck, I'm like, what would nature do? Right? An example would be Boston; this is a mature economy; it's a mature ecosystem. A hardwood forest in New England grows at a rate of 3 to 4 percent a year; it doesn't grow faster than that. That seems like a good reasonable rate to set my returns at. A bamboo forest grows at a rate of 35 percent a year, colonizes everything in its path, destroys all subspecies, and that sounds a little bit to me like Wall Street. So that's what I mean by, can biomimicry—can nature give me some insight? It's this fantastic system that seems to work really well and stick around unless we do something to it. So, when I get stuck, that's where I turn for insight.

You can watch the full interview with Deborah here: deborah.s4g.biz.

Deborah Frieze is a Boston-based impact investor who manages a fund focusing on addressing racial disparities there. She notes that the city is on par with Atlanta for average net worth differences between white versus African American households. The former group reports average household wealth of $247,000 while Black ones have an average of $8. Not $8,000. Just eight dollars.

Her strategy at Boston Impact Initiative Fund is to help African American entrepreneurs access more affordable capital. Unfortunately, the impact investment community has typically taken an approach that, similar to the broader financial market, favors the interests of investors over entrepreneurs.

Deborah observed that this model perpetuates rather than reversing the wealth disparities. Investors, almost by definition, have money. Entrepreneurs need it. As a result, investors typically are better positioned to absorb risk than those they back. Still, impact investors often use structures that focus on reducing risk and increasing return for the investors.

Boston Impact Initiative Fund reverses that through innovative structures that employ grant capital to reduce borrowing costs for entrepreneurs and require wealthy and institutional investors to accept greater risk.

No matter how sensible this sounds to you, it is essential to understand that to traditional investment bankers, it seems as reasonable as cats barking or fish flying.

Deborah is working to spool up her work in Boston to serve more people. At the same time, communities across the country are working with her to replicate what she's doing to help underserved entrepreneurs.

It is fascinating that biomimicry is the root of this innovation. At the top of this chapter, Deborah explained how she uses nature as a model for finance in her own words. Biomimicry is a growing discipline across industries. Before connecting with her, I couldn't have imagined it would have application in finance. Her use suggests there may be few limits to the application of her superpower.

How to Develop Biomimicry as a Superpower

Learning how to apply biomimicry in your life is likely a bit different from being more optimistic. You already know a lot about optimism, even if you could use a bit more. You may be reading about biomimicry for the first time.

If you want to go deep, consider reading Deborah's book *Walk Out Walk On*.

There are some simple steps you can take immediately to begin using biomimicry.

1. *Get into nature.* You can likely find ways to spend more time in nature. Go incrementally. If you're a typical urbanite like me, it may begin simply by going outside. Move to spend more time in open spaces like parks. You may be able to move part of your exercise routine from the gym to the outdoors. Perhaps you can switch some of your travel from city destinations to rural or wild ones. For safety reasons, be sure to inch forward. Before seeking to spend a week in the wilds of Alaska or summiting Mount Kilimanjaro, try going for a walk or hike nearer your home. Some quiet time alone in nature can lead to insights you might discover no other way. But being alone can also be a good strategy for finding trouble. Take a friend or hire a guide when you go to new places in nature.
2. *Learn about nature.* There are countless resources available for learning about nature. Find the ones that fit your learning style. Do you love documentary films? Watch more about nature. Do you love books? Read more about biology. Do you love podcasts? Listen to some about wilderness. Regardless of how you like to learn, plan to include more about nature in your study. What you learn from your research will complement what you learn outdoors.
3. *Practice.* As you spend more time in nature and learning about it, you can begin applying biomimicry to your life. Begin by identifying simple questions in your daily life and looking for biological answers. For instance, you may wonder if there is a way to incorporate fun into your daily routines. As you watch squirrels in the park or even insects in the grass, you will sometimes see them at play, despite the life and death struggle the great outdoors represents. You may be able to find lessons there. As you practice,

as with any skill, you'll get better at finding the models and applying them to your work, personal life and relationships.

Biomimicry can be a formal discipline, like engineering, that becomes the focus of how you spend your days or just a fresh perspective for seeing facts in a new light. Whichever you choose, by taking these simple steps, you can begin to make it one of your superpowers.

Bill Drayton

Chapter 19: Changemaking - Bill Drayton

Devin: *What is your superpower?*

Bill: *One looks at roots. I had two parents who did crazy things when they were 19. They had in them a comfort with me doing things, and they were supportive. I grew up in Manhattan, so there was no station wagon prison. There was a free bus and subway pass once you're allowed to cross the street. And it was the time of the civil rights movement. I couldn't stand all this memorization stuff. And so I didn't do it very much. I loved history and geography, but math and French, please! And you can tell I'm not built for contact sport. I'm always the crashee, which limited my enthusiasm for it. So I started a newspaper, and it became a newspaper that grew and grew and grew. Once I was able to buy a mimeograph machine, which I bet you very few people have any idea what that technology is.*

Devin: *I'm married to a school teacher. I'm very familiar with it.*

Bill: *Well, that was open sesame for me. And you know, I had a principal who I learned, many years later, he prevented conflict. He reassured—even my parents needed reassurance. That was just a huge gift. So we all have to understand the roots of this. I was given the gift of being able to imagine and go and do things and build things. Every time you do that, you get better at it, and you're able to give at a bigger level and help more people grow more. This is very contagious.*

You can watch the full interview with Bill at bill.s4g.biz.

Bill Drayton founded Ashoka more than 40 years ago, after a remarkable career that culminated with a senior position in the Carter Administration. Educated at Harvard, Oxford and Yale, he was positioned for greatness. He chose to become the changemaker who sponsors, teaches and mentors other changemakers. His impact on the planet—on humanity—is now incalculable.

When Bill founded Ashoka to support social entrepreneurs, he coined the term changemaker, now in everyday use, referring to people who drive social change. The Oxford Dictionary added the word nearly a decade ago, a point of pride for Bill. However, Webster still defines changemaker only as the device that gives change in a cash transaction, a point of contention for him.

Ashoka has formally supported nearly 4,000 Ashoka Fellows, social entrepreneurs who receive financial and other support.

"Over half of these Ashoka Fellows change national policy within five years of launch, and three-quarters have created systems change in their field at the national or international levels," Ashoka reports.

The ripples from Bill's work extend so far that countless people influenced by his efforts don't realize he is the source. They are busy working for change and likely haven't applied for a fellowship or received direct support from Ashoka. Instead, without realizing it, they have followed the example of an Ashoka fellow, been inspired by something they've written or even been financed by one.

Put another way, it would be difficult to find a person on the planet who has not been impacted somehow by one of the ripples extending out from Bill's choice 40 years ago to launch Ashoka.

Today, Bill recognizes that a centuries-long trend is reaching a critical point. The rate of change is accelerating. He sees the beginning of this shift at about the year 1700. Whenever it began, experts agree that the trend is reaching a challenging level.

Individuals cannot reasonably expect to have a single career span over 40 years. To be clear, I'm not saying you can't expect to start a job at one company at 25 and retire at 65 from that company. In fact, that has been true for a generation. What is changing now is that with the rate of change accelerating, most people will have to switch not jobs, not companies, but to entirely new careers.

Bill argues that the only way to succeed in this fast-changing world is to lead the change. Therefore, everyone must learn to be a changemaker.

You can learn to make changemaking a superpower.

How to Develop Changemaking as a Superpower

When I asked Bill about his superpower, he labeled it "roots." He was talking about how his parents and his principal at school enabled him to learn, explore, and ultimately become a young changemaker as a teenage newspaper publisher.

When we spoke, he explained how to teach children to be changemakers. It may be more challenging for adults to learn these skills because they take us outside our comfort zone. Nevertheless, you can learn to be a changemaker.

He advises parents to help children become changemakers by following a simple pattern.

1. *Recognize a problem.* When your 12-year-old comes to you with a social problem of any sort—kids struggling to learn math or accept a trans friend—your first task is to celebrate the recognition of a challenging issue. Give your child your complete attention.
2. *Challenge the problem.* Having recognized the issue, encourage your child to think about how to fix it. Bill warns against giving ideas. Remember, you're teaching your child to become a changemaker.
3. *Repeat.* Your child is unlikely to come back with an idea to solve this problem. Don't fret. They will be back with another problem someday. When that happens, repeat the steps above. Repeat patiently.
4. *Encourage.* When they do come back with an idea to address a problem, be encouraging but don't take over. Don't let an older sibling or teacher take over. Let them lead the way with their friends to create a solution.

The logic is clear enough for children. You can see how Bill's parents, as he describes them as "having done crazy things when they were 19," were giving him this sort of implicit training. He's taking his lived experience to provide you with a way to teach your children to become changemakers while they are still forming social patterns and defining their comfort zone.

As an adult, you have arrived at this point with your own comfort zone that may or may not include leading change. If not, you can modify the four steps above to your own life and circumstance so you can learn to be a changemaker.

1. *Recognize a problem.* When you see a problem, celebrate the observation. Next, decide if this problem deserves your attention. If not, move on until you see another problem. If it does merit your attention, move to step two.
2. *Challenge the problem.* Give some thought to how you, with your network, resources and skills, can make a difference. If a problem deserves your attention, you can make a difference in solving it. Don't give up.
3. *Implement your solution.* After you define a plan for solving the problem, implement it. There is nothing wrong with seeking help. The reason you don't take over for your kids is so they learn to lead. That doesn't mean that when you are leading a solution, you don't need help. You do. Ask for it. Implement your solution.
4. *Repeat.* When the problem is solved, return to step one.

Bill has some additional insight for learning to be a changemaker. "Start with cognitive empathy."

"When you say the word empathy, typically people think, 'put yourself in other people's shoes, feel someone else's pain,' whatever," Bill explains. "That's a part of it. That's your mirror neurons. That's early brain. That's very, very important. But you have to have the other part: the cerebral cortex."

You need to thoughtfully comprehend another's situation by using both your ability to feel what they are experiencing and understand it as well as possible.

Next, he emphasizes a need for complicated teamwork. "It's not Henry Ford having an idea and telling thousands of people to repeat for the next 50 decades," he quips. Instead, you've got to be able to lead one minute and play another role at another.

With those two skills, cognitive empathy and complicated teamwork, you can construct a more fluid architecture for your idea to spread naturally.

Let's be honest with each other. Most people won't achieve the level of impact that Bill has. One thing is for sure, however: the ones who will are those willing to try. If you're eager to make an effort, it makes sense to draw on the lessons of the consummate changemaker to see if you can make it your superpower, too.

Sam Daley-Harris

Chapter 20: Confidence in Collective Action - Sam Daley-Harris

Devin: What is your superpower?

Sam: What is my superpower?

I think it's that I'm in on the joke. I actually know that people can make a difference, and I keep my eye on that ball.

I look at the news, and I get a little depressed by the news. But I look at what the grassroots groups I am working with are doing, and I get excited. Last year [President Trump] called for a 31 percent cut to the Global Fund to Fight AIDS Tuberculosis and Malaria, which over the last 17 years, along with its partners, had saved 27 million lives. Results volunteers got 162 Republicans and Democrats to sign one letter to the top appropriators on the subcommittee that appropriates it saying, no, don't cut it. The appropriations subcommittee has nine people on it. When those nine subcommittee members get a letter signed by 162 [of their Congressional colleagues] saying pay attention to the Global Fund to Fight AIDS, [it matters]. So I pay attention to those volunteers who are getting 162 Republicans and Democrats to say no, don't cut the Global Fund to Fight AIDS, Tuberculosis and Malaria. When I look at the Citizens' Climate Lobby, last year, they had enrolled 45 Republicans and 45 Democrats in the House Climate Solutions caucus when four years ago you couldn't get one Republican to put their name on anything with the word climate in the title. How exciting does that get about breakthroughs in new territory! So, I'm in on the joke that people think, somebody thinks, everybody thinks we can't make a difference [on big issues]. I know that we can. And I keep my eye on the ball [and on all of those who are making a difference.] That really feeds me.

You can watch the full interview with Sam here: sam.s4g.biz.

Sam Daley-Harris may be the most impactful person you've never heard of. He runs with the likes of Nobel Peace Prize Laureate Muhammad Yunus. Trained as a musician, Sam founded RESULTS, a leading anti-poverty lobby that deserves credit for dramatically reducing child mortality globally over the past 40 years.

He first began asking questions about his purpose when a friend died in 1964. He was further shaken by the assassination of Robert Kennedy in 1968, again causing him to ponder the question of his purpose.

In 1977, he attended a presentation on ending world hunger. Up to that point, he had assumed that if ending world hunger were possible, it would have happened. So, clearly, it wasn't. He learned some unsurprising facts that changed his thinking. There is no mystery to growing or distributing food. The problem was simply creating the will to end hunger. The event planted a seed of confidence—hope—that collective action could change things.

Sam jumped in with both feet. Classroom by classroom, he spoke to 7,000 high school students about fighting global hunger. In every presentation, he asked the students if they could name their congressional representative. Only 3 percent could! From this disappointment, he saw an opportunity.

Because so few people are aware of and are engaging with their representatives in Washington, he figured out that they could make a big difference by organizing a small group of people. He saw that a systematic approach could change policies that would save lives. The approach included writing letters to the editor and opinion pieces for newspapers to shape public opinion and directly lobbying members of Congress through letters, phone calls and personal visits.

In 1980, he founded RESULTS to do just that. In those 41 years, the number of children dying from hunger and preventable disease has dropped from 41,000 to 14,000 per day. There is still work to do, but millions of people are alive today because governments, responding to pressure from citizens, have funded efforts to end hunger.

Along the way, Sam's confidence in the power of collective action, the unstoppable force of a citizen-led campaign for change, became absolute.

In 2007, he helped Marshall Saunders, founder of Citizens' Climate Lobby, organize a parallel effort for fighting climate change. Muhammad Yunus now sits on the board. Today, the organization boasts over 180,000 members in 590 groups around the world. Sam is confident that this effort will help to reverse climate change.

How to Develop Confidence in Collective Action as a Superpower

Let's not belabor a simple plan. When I spoke with Sam for this book, he said the best way to gain confidence in collective action is to participate and practice. You can watch that interview at sam2.s4g.biz.

Sam shared with me the story of Marshall Saunders's first meeting with a member of Congress. Marshall was so nervous that he couldn't remember what he had prepared to say. Now, it is routine. Citizens' Climate Lobby members, including Marshall, met with 1,800 members of Congress and their staff members in a single year. Practice makes progress and builds confidence.

Sam notes that it is essential to join a group that will empower you as an advocate. Some organizations designed to lobby Congress use a different approach, focused on collecting money from donors to pay Washington lobbyists to push the agenda. Others, like RESULTS and Citizens' Climate Lobby, empower and encourage their members to use their voices.

When you join an empowering group, you will receive training on writing letters to the editor and OpEds that will get published. You'll get coaching on writing letters to members of Congress that will get read. You'll even have opportunities to join with your peers to visit the halls of Congress and meet with your representatives to make your case. As you experience this, you will gain confidence in the power of collective action to make a significant difference in the world.

Dr. Ujala Nayyar courtesy of Rotary International

Chapter 21: Coping with Stress - Dr. Ujala Nayyar

Devin: What is your superpower?

Dr. Ujala: Work under stress. I manage. I don't panic. Because there are conditions—because, for example, from my program, I have the largest number of AFP [acute flaccid paralysis, possible polio] cases across Pakistan. Last year we had [thousands of] cases—AFP cases. So then there are conditions when we receive calls, immediately send this! Send this! Send this! So, managing the stress and still staying calm is the best quality I have. That's my superpower.

You can watch the full interview with Dr. Ujala here: ujala.s4g.biz.

Dr. Ujala Nayyar leads the World Health Organization's polio surveillance effort in Pakistan, one of only two countries in the world where the disease continues to paralyze children. She is a crucial person in bringing a global end to polio once and for all.

Rotary International initiated the fight to eradicate polio in partnership with the U.S. Centers for Disease Control (CDC) in the mid-1980s. UNICEF and the World Health Organization quickly joined the effort, collectively forming the Global Polio Eradication Initiative. The Gates Foundation became the chief funder of the initiative and a full partner in the early 2000s.

In the mid-1980s, there were about 350,000 cases of polio each year. In 2017, there were just 22 cases of polio caused by the wild poliovirus—all in Pakistan and Afghanistan, representing a 99.99 percentage reduction. However, various challenges, including the pandemic, have led to an increase in cases since. But as I write this, the year 2021 shows encouraging data that suggests a return to declining case counts and hope for prompt and complete eradication.

In India, in 2009, there were 741 cases of polio. In 2010, just 42. The last case of polio in that enormous country occurred in January 2011. Rotary International invited me to observe some of the celebrations of the 2014 declaration of the country as officially polio-free. My takeaway from that observance is that eradication can happen relatively quickly when everything comes together. So, I hope we'll be surprised by Dr. Ujala's ultimate success soon.

In addition to her work on polio, Dr. Ujala serves as an essential role model for women and what we could call an object lesson for men in Pakistan. This is because she has a position of authority and prestige. Yet, many women in Pakistan are treated unequally by men and the government. She experiences "negative vibes" and subtle discrimination, she says. "I am privileged by my birth but not by my society."

As a female leader on the polio eradication team in Pakistan, the eradication of this disease which has been around throughout human history, will be cause for congratulations from the entire globe, most particularly perhaps, women in her country.

With all that hangs in the balance of her work, it is hard to imagine the stress she feels. Bill Gates follows her efforts closely, as do other polio fighters around the world. Those who survive polio, almost always children, typically have their lives irreparably altered by it. Most were living in difficult situations before contracting the disease. They clamor for help. As a mother herself, Dr. Ujala feels for the children who suffer and their mothers. As a result, her role puts her in the center of a stress hurricane. Her superpower, coping with stress, is essential for her success.

How to Develop Coping with Stress as a Superpower

You likely feel stress. Most people do. As I write this during a global pandemic, there is evidence of higher pressure for everyone globally. The virus added another significant risk factor, and governments responding added various new regulations that impact everyone. One symptom: as passengers return to air travel, an epidemic of mistreating flight crews is erupting.

Small amounts of stress can be good for you. Still, too much stress can harm your health and your happiness. There are some ways you can see if the pressure is beginning to overwhelm your ability to cope. Check this list[7] to see if you recognize these symptoms:

- Prolonged periods of poor sleep
- Regular, severe headaches
- Unexplained weight loss or gain
- Feelings of isolation, withdrawal or worthlessness
- Constant anger and irritability
- Loss of interest in activities
- Constant worrying or obsessive thinking
- Excessive alcohol or drug use
- Inability to concentrate

If you see yourself in the above list, take action immediately. The CDC[8] offers five tips for coping with stress.

1. *Take care of yourself.* Eat healthy, exercise, get plenty of sleep, and give yourself a break if you feel stressed out.
2. *Talk to others.* Share your problems and feelings with a parent, friend, counselor, doctor or clergy.
3. *Avoid drugs and alcohol.* These may seem to help, but they can create additional problems and increase the stress you are already feeling.
4. *Take a news break.* If news events are causing you stress, take a break from listening or watching the news.
5. *Recognize when you need more help.* If problems continue or you are thinking about suicide, talk to a psychologist, social worker or professional counselor.

If the stress in your life comes primarily from work, you may also want to consider the tips in Chapter 17 on Balance.

Even if you don't find yourself ready to jump into the center of a stress hurricane, you can keep yourself healthy and keep working to make a difference in the world by assessing your reaction to stress and actively managing it. Coping with stress can become your superpower.

---

[7] Malaika Stoll, M.D., Sutter Health, "10 Simple Ways to Cope with Stress," https://www.sutterhealth.org/health/mind-body/10-simple-ways-to-cope-with-stress.

[8] Centers for Disease Control, "Coping with Stress," https://www.cdc.gov/violenceprevention/about/copingwith-stresstips.html.

Warner Woodworth by Anna Nalbandyan

Chapter 22: Disruption - Warner Woodworth

Devin: *Warner, what is your superpower?*

Warner: *I don't have stuff like that. I avoid superhero movies, or my grandkids want me to go see that stuff. I say that's all fake. I don't think there's any kind of superpower I have.*

Devin: *What makes you successful?*

Warner: *Well, I suppose I'm a disruptor. I'm a change agent. I tell my classes at the beginning of every semester, "You're not here to call me Dr. Woodworth or Heir Professor or Brother Woodworth in the Mormon Church. Just call me Warner. I'm a student like you. We're all scholars; we're all trying to learn together."*

"And I'm going to try to disrupt your paradigm and challenge your assumptions. And I'm going to hope as a renegade, I kind of shake you up a bit—and be a catalyst to help you find a more authentic life and a great future that's not going to be just a job—because that's not enough during your 60, 70, 80, 90 years on this earth. I want you to figure

out how you can be an agent for transformation. And I'm here to help empower you to do that. And hopefully, we can together build a sense of community."

So those kinds of values and those kinds of motivations, along with a huge component of high ethics and commitment to social justice and peace. Those are the values that are pretty much burned into my brain and into my heart.

You can watch the full interview with Warner here: warner.s4g.biz.

Warner Woodworth is not your typical business school professor, much less what you'd expect from Brigham Young University's Marriott School of Management. A champion of the underserved, he's spent his career teaching students and helping others to build social enterprises and nonprofit organizations. He has a genuine disdain for greed.

Over his career, he has helped form dozens of nonprofits and social enterprises, including Unitus, one of the early players in microfinance. He advocated for making loans to women with no income in remote and rural locations around the world before he heard of or befriended Nobel Laureate Muhammad Yunus.

By way of an example, he shares the story of Maria, a woman in Honduras who was part of a group of women whose lives and livelihoods had been devastated by Hurricane Mitch in 1998. He helped them organize a microloan fund. When presented with the cash for a $100 loan to help her start a small personal business, she responded crying that she wasn't "worthy." She didn't believe she could pay it back. "I've never seen so much money," she said.

Warner believed in Maria. With tears in his eyes, he said, "You can do this. We love you. We trust you. We know this will work."

Maria accepted the funds and launched a small chicken farm, initially with 12 chickens. Within a year, she had 5,000 chickens. She was worthy. She was capable. He saw it before she did, but she was the one who executed well and performed the transformation.

Warner teaches his students to use disruption to become "positive deviants." He says that the folks he has helped create microfinance companies have funded 20 million businesses, about 99 percent founded by women. The borrowers overwhelmingly repay their loans. Disruption works.

How to Develop Disruption as a Superpower

Warner says you have a choice. You can stay on the freeway with a successful American life, recycling and reciprocating conventional wisdom, or you can make a definitive decision to shake up the status quo.

Warner joined me for a follow-up conversation mainly focused on how you can learn disruption. You can watch it here: woodworth.s4g.biz.

No matter what other strengths you may have, you can add some disruption to increase the impact of what you're doing. Here are the seven tips that Warner shared for learning to be a positive deviant.

1. *Shake up the status quo.* Something about the situation you are in is not working, or you wouldn't want to change it. To change outcomes, it is likely you need to change the system. Warner says, "I started my career with an explicit goal to shake up the status quo." He didn't want to make tweaks; he wanted to make a difference. That's a worthy goal.

2. *Start bottom-up.* While Warner acknowledges that large NGOs from the Federal Government to the Gates Foundation do great work, it is difficult to disrupt what's happening there. At the bottom, in the urban streets or jungle trails into villages, are opportunities to help people in entirely new and novel ways.

3. *Innovate.* "Do something innovative and a little crazy," he says. Conventional wisdom often seeks to replicate what works. Warner says disruptors start something new, bring a fresh approach or see a problem that others have ignored.

4. *Start small.* One of the patterns Warner cautions against is the desire to start something at scale. He says it is critical to prove the concept works before you begin to scale. He often helps those he mentors find a donor or build a small advisory board to help fine-tune the plan. The team of backers and doers still fit in one living room.

5. *Pace your growth.* One of Warner's efforts is helping several worker-owned businesses in the Basque region of Spain, which have become some of the most successful in Europe. They told him, "We build the road as we travel." This observation is good guidance for growing your impact-oriented effort. You want to be sure not to get too far out in front of the people you hope to help.

6. *Gather data.* Another critical step, the professor says, is to be sure to document your progress and record your data. Records will help you attract additional support as you demonstrate the impact of your work. Ultimately, you are doing this to make a

difference in the world. It is wise to begin measuring the difference you make from the earliest days.

7. *Hire locals.* As you scale up the operation, one of your priorities should be hiring local people in the community within the country to lead the effort. Your goal should be to create a home-grown operation that you support rather than an international operation with foreigners imposing their will on vulnerable communities.

Warner makes clear that his advice doesn't apply only to traditional students. He notes that many people today are discovering in their 50s that they can retire and have the longevity to expect to live into their 90s, giving them 20 to 30 years of productive post-employment opportunity.

"You don't need to stay in this big mansion. You don't need to live in a luxurious condo. You don't need to check your income every day and look at increased revenues. You can think about finding new purpose, a kind of a purpose-driven life," Warner says. "You could consider doing something radically different and have a whole new life, kind of like a rebirth for the next 20, 30 years."

In other words, you can start by disrupting your own life.

Jessica Rolph

Chapter 23: Entrepreneurship - Jessica Rolph

Devin: *Jessica, what is your superpower?*

Jessica: *Believing in something. There were so many years— six years of incubation with my first baby—where I was trying out all these products. I was teaching him lessons about heavy and light and trying to come up with examples. I was making my own fabric tissue boxes and books. I had these dreams as I was incubating and wanting to take that next step to make it real. I was persisting throughout the emotional ups and downs. If we're speaking to entrepreneurs—and I know a lot of your followers are entrepreneurs—there are so many ups and downs. I'm good at disengaging my emotions and saying, "what is the very next step that I need to take to make this real?" whether I feel excited about it or I'm completely worried about it. Because before something is out in the world, it's vulnerable. Lovevery is a result of all these lessons that I tried with my own children that are now real. I couldn't have this with my children when they were young, so instead, I had to make it. Now, it's so fun to be able to give to other children. I think being able to make something real is the superpower.*

You can watch the full interview with Jessica and president and co-founder Rod Morris here: jessica.s4g.biz.

Jessica Rolph is the consummate entrepreneur. She was part of the founding team at Happy Family, an organic food business that started making baby food. Group Danone bought the startup for a rumored $250 million. With that success, she founded a venture-backed educational toy company called Lovevery.

Like the heavy and light balls she mentioned when describing her superpower, she designed the products using the best science she could find. Her goal is to help other parents begin teaching their children almost from birth.

By researching the right age for each lesson, the company created a schedule of new books and toys for babies and toddlers to begin learning. Typically, Lovevery sells its products via a subscription tied to the baby's birth, so relevant products for each stage of development arrive at the customer's door periodically.

During the development phase, Lovevery gathered insights from parents across the economic spectrum and found a universal desire to help their kids learn and develop optimally.

As a parent herself, Jessica was motivated in part by the desire to help her own children. She describes the process of bringing products to market as "making something real" and identifies it as her superpower. As I've watched her grow two startups, I think it is fair to describe her superpower as entrepreneurship. It isn't having the tangible thing in her hand that excites her; it is having the ability to sell it to every interested parent on the planet.

Happy Family was an entrepreneurial home run. Lovevery is on its way. As one who has helped create two businesses that have scaled as hers have, she's exceptional. But she isn't all about the money either. Both her companies include a social mission. Frankly, she's my kind of business leader: a social entrepreneur.

How to Develop Entrepreneurship as a Superpower

Who wouldn't want to be as successful as Jessica? There is a lot you can learn from her. Applying even some of the lessons she gives you can improve your ability to innovate and grow what you're doing.

From my conversations with Jessica, company president and co-founder Rod, and others regarding Lovevery, I've gleaned five lessons for entrepreneurship you can apply.

1. *Invest your time.* Jessica spent about six years between having the first idea and selling the first Lovevery product. She was raising her son and began thinking about ideas for toys that could be developed and sold to parents like her.
2. *Do your research.* Especially for products like these—baby toys—it would be tempting to use your intuition and experience as a parent as the only guide for creating products. Her decision to use thoughtful research into the science both helped her build better products and attracted the early venture capitalists who backed her.
3. *Partner.* Jessica learned the lesson well. As a founding team member at Happy Family, she knew not to go it alone as an entrepreneur at Lovevery. She found Rod had a perfect background and enthusiastically shared her vision for the educational toy venture. He joined as the co-founder and president.
4. *Dig a moat.* Lovevery has gone beyond just using sound science to develop products. They have used competent lawyers to file at least four patents, protecting the business. Seeking intellectual property protection, including patents, is sometimes described as digging a moat. It creates a barrier for competitors allowing you a bit of extra room for growth.
5. *Find big markets.* There is nothing wrong with building a business for a small market. You probably have a favorite restaurant, boutique or other local small business that is important to you. The world would be poorer without them. Still, if you want to do the most good, reach the most people, and, yes, make the most money, you'll want to copy Jessica's model for finding big markets. In both businesses, she targeted parents of babies, recognizing that there are millions of babies in the world.

These tips don't represent a complete guide to entrepreneurship, but if you've got a business idea, following these tips can help you get closer to Jessica's level of success. Even if you don't choose to make entrepreneurship your superpower, you can see how her example can help you do other aspects of your work better.

Liz Scott

Chapter 24: Gratitude - Liz Scott

Devin: *Liz, what is your superpower?*

Liz: *I would say, if this counts as a superpower, probably gratitude. To get through something really hard in life, as we went through with Alex and losing Alex, you have to be able to feel grateful. You have to be able to feel grateful for what you have currently and to feel grateful for what you had. And with any loss, it's really important to feel as though the loss of the person doesn't take away from the greatness while they were here. Right? And it's the greatness you want to remember and be thankful for. And it's the loss you want to try to fill up with positive things in gratitude for what you do have in your life.*

You can watch my interviews with Liz here: liz1.s4g.biz and liz2.s4g.biz.

Liz Scott is the mother of Alex Scott, the little girl who launched a lemonade stand to cure cancer. The lemonade stand became Alex's Lemonade Stand Foundation and is now a player in a global race to end the insidious disease.

When I first interviewed Liz, I was an emotional wreck. While I'm a bit of a softy, and you can find me on occasion drying a tear during an interview, none were like this one. Taking what she told me and what I could learn from talking to others impacted by Liz and Alex, I prepared this retelling of the story.

Right now, my four-year-old cousin Simon is fighting for his life at Salt Lake's Primary Children's Hospital. Chances are, you know a child who is battling or has battled cancer.

I want to tell you a story that gives me hope for Simon.

Alex Scott was born a fighter. She arrived prematurely in 1996 and demonstrated her tenacity immediately, defying the odds and quickly earning the right to leave the hospital. Her mother, Liz, says it was a "glimpse" of what was to come.

Before her first birthday, Alex was diagnosed with neuroblastoma—Simon's cancer.

Liz says, "Everything they had they threw at her."

When she had a bad day, she would find a way to get through it with grace.

The doctors tried all the conventional therapies, chemo, radiation and surgery. Nothing worked.

So, they started experimental treatments. One, Metaiodobenzylguanidine or MIBG therapy, allowed them to perform a stem cell transplant.

Even before it was confirmed by the CAT scans, Alex told her parents the therapy was working.

Then, in January of 2000, she told her mom she wanted to do a lemonade stand. Given the weather in Connecticut at that time of year—not to mention that they were a little preoccupied caring for a cancer patient—her mom put her off.

In June, Alex, then four and half years old, said, "I still haven't had my stand."

Annoyed, her mother asked, "Alex, what do you want to buy so badly that you need to have this lemonade stand?"

"I'm not keeping the money; I'm giving it to my doctors so they can help kids the way they helped me."

And so, Alex's Lemonade Stand was born.

By the time she was six, she'd raised about $30,000. Her parents were giving the money exclusively to fund neuroblastoma research to find a cure for Alex's cancer.

When Alex found out, she said, "That is so selfish."

Her mom wanted to say, "I don't care!"

Before she could get the words out, Alex said, "All kids want their cancer to go away. We should be giving money to all hospitals for all kinds of cancer." That statement has defined the nonprofit's vision ever since.

Alex's Lemonade Stand Foundation has now funded research on 25 different pediatric cancers.

Well, by age eight, Alex knew the treatments had stopped working. So, she was going to have one last stand and thought if everybody helped, if everybody had lemonade stands on the same day as hers, they could raise $1 million.

"She held on to see that goal met. She died knowing that she had accomplished this seemingly insurmountable [ambition]."

After Alex passed away, the Scotts weren't sure they would continue the fundraising effort. Alex really was the driving force.

But other people kept supporting the cause.

"How could you walk away from the opportunity to help other children?" Liz said.

So, the work continues. As a result, real progress has been made, especially over the past ten years. She says she regularly hears from parents now who say their child has been in remission for one year, two years, three years. It is "indescribable" to think that Alex's life has had that effect, Liz says.

Liz remains personally connected to the families of children with cancer even as the organization grows in scale and impact. "It's both inspiring and really hard because a lot of them do really well. And some of them don't."

For the most common cancers, there are several treatment options. But, for families facing a rare cancer, there may be only one standard treatment—for some rare cancers, there are none.

It is for these families that Liz is most optimistic. She thinks curing cancer is realistic. Today's progress is smart progress, she says. We're looking at immunotherapies, targeted therapies and personalized medicine. That's how every child will have the possibility of a cure.

Liz confesses, "When Alex said she was going to cure cancer with the lemonade stand, honestly, I thought it was cute, and I was proud. [But] I didn't think it would make a big difference in the world of fighting cancer."

She couldn't have been more wrong. Today, Alex would be 21. The tally of lives saved and extended by her Foundation is beginning to mount. By the time Alex would normally have reached middle age, a childhood cancer diagnosis may be no more threatening than a cold.

Alex lost her battle with cancer, but the organization she founded as a four-year-old selling lemonade in the front yard has gone on to raise over $150 million.

Alex won the war—for Simon.

Four years have passed since I wrote this, and the total raised is over $200 million.

And my Simon is cancer-free.

When you think about the money raised and the people who gave it, it is not so hard to understand Liz's superpower: gratitude. But, on the other hand, when you think about the pain and suffering Alex endured without ever really having a chance to grow up, you begin to wonder how she could feel grateful.

Twice, more than two years apart, I asked Liz about her superpower, and she responded the same way each time. She is grateful. And it is her core strength.

How to Develop Gratitude as a Superpower

Liz's story inspires me. I hope it inspires you, too. I am grateful for her willingness to share her story with me and you. I'm thankful that her work is saving children's lives.

In our interviews, Liz explained the importance of gratitude in the face of tragic loss.

First, Liz suggests that gratitude can help you cope with loss. I would not have jumped to that conclusion, but she said, "To get through something really hard in life, as we went through with Alex and losing Alex, you have to be able to feel grateful. You have to be able to feel grateful for what you have currently and to feel grateful for what you had."

Everyone has had significant losses. Feeling gratitude for what you had and lost strikes me as a profound life lesson.

Beyond coping with the loss, Liz suggests that gratitude motivates her to "fill up with positive things." Raising $200 million to fight childhood cancer is a pretty positive thing.

The University of Minnesota provides a list of tips for increasing gratitude in your life.[9] Here are some highlights.

1. *Say three things.* Every day, say aloud three things you're grateful happened that day—even if you're alone.

---

[9] Andrea Uptmor, University of Minnesota, Earl E. Bakken Center for Spirituality and Healing, "10 Ways to Be a More Thankful Person,"

2. *Keep a journal.* In it, focus on writing down the things you are grateful to have, to have had or to have experienced. On bad days, review your notes.

3. *Thank your partner.* Couples that express appreciation to one another are happier.

4. *Stop when angry.* Before reacting to a situation that has triggered your anger, think of five things you're grateful for. It will cool your anger and allow you to approach the problem more constructively.

5. *Thank yourself.* You rock. You take care of yourself. Acknowledge yourself with gratitude for the good you do.

6. *Text a thank-you.* Once a day, think of someone to thank and send a quick text to express it. Just a moment will make a difference in your life and someone else's, too.

7. *Look for silver linings.* Whenever something unfortunate happens, remember it could be worse. Then, look for the benefits that might come from the challenge—even if it is a simple reminder that what doesn't kill you makes you stronger.

You can make gratitude a superpower. By following Liz's example and these ideas, you can be more effective in your work and happier in your life.

Philippe Cousteau and Ashlan Cousteau

Chapter 25: Knowing What You Don't Know - Philippe Cousteau

Devin: *Philippe, what's your superpower?*

Philippe: *I know what I don't know. I think that's very important. We always say that "know what you don't know." We don't have all the answers. Really be willing to work and surround yourself with smart people who do have the answers and listen to them. Hubris is a terrible thing, and I think too many of our leaders suffer from that affliction. And it's very important, I believe, to work with other people who enhance you and you can enhance them. And be willing to say, "I have no idea." But never give up in terms of trying to find the answer. No matter how or who it takes to help you to do that.*

You can watch the full interview with Philippe here: phil.s4g.biz.

Philippe Cousteau, founder of the nonprofit educational organization EarthEcho International, and television sea explorer, follows in the footsteps—er wake—of his famous grandfather Jacques Cousteau.

Philippe is a multi-Emmy Award nominee television host. He hosts Awesome Planet for Fox and Hulu, he is a special correspondent for CNN and, with his wife Ashlan, he is the co-host of Caribbean Pirate Treasure for the Travel Channel.

With his sister Alexandra, Philippe co-founded EarthEcho, which focuses on empowering youth to become environmental changemakers. The siblings see this effort as a way to honor their late father, Philippe Cousteau, Sr., and grandfather. "Our mission is to inspire young people worldwide to act now for a sustainable future," they say.

He expressed frustration that environmental protection has become politically divisive. "I always like to remind people that Richard Nixon passed the Clean Air Act, the Clean Water Act and the Marine Mammal Protection Act. He founded the EPA," Philippe says. "We can argue about foreign policy; we can argue about economic policy; when it comes right down to it, clean air and clean water are non-negotiable."

During my Congressional campaign, Philippe joined me for a second episode of my show, this time with his co-star and wife Ashlan. You can watch that interview here: ashlan.s4g.biz.

In addition to advocacy for environmental protection, EarthEcho provides educational content, which increasingly provides a bridge from the environment to STEM (science, technology, engineering and math) skills. This connection helps students think about careers where they can earn a living even as they continue to protect the sea and the life it supports.

"What better way to study biology, chemistry and engineering than nature because that's where it all comes from," Philippe says.

Given his focus on learning and education, I was startled a bit by his superpower, knowing what you don't know. It takes courage to acknowledge limits. To describe that trait as a superpower struck me initially as the equivalent of calling kryptonite one. On further reflection, however, you can see how it is empowering. You can master this, too.

How to Develop Knowing What You Don't Know as a Superpower

To learn how to identify what you don't know may sound easy, even if humbling, but that's not quite right. It is relatively easy to acknowledge you don't know everything but figuring out what you don't know takes work.

If you want to do something you've never done, you're going to need help. If you're going to do something that no one has ever done—something changemakers have to do from time to time—you're going to need a lot of help. Your challenge is to determine what guidance, support and education you need.

We live in a great age. Answers to simple questions are just a Google search or YouTube video away. But sometimes, you need a level of expertise or skill you can't glean quickly enough from the internet.

As you seek to change the world, consider the following tips to help you optimize knowing what you don't know.

1. *Identify gaps early.* Philippe would be in real trouble if he realized he didn't know something critical to his production once he found himself on the bottom of the ocean. Recognizing a lack of knowledge too late would be especially problematic if the answer was equipment only available on the other side of the world. So, you've got to assess what you may need early in your timeline.
2. *Study.* Knowing what you don't know actually requires you to know a lot. For example, say you're a Ph.D. biologist who needs a website. The more you know about internet technology, the easier it will be to figure out where you need help. Without a foundational understanding of web design and function, you may not realize that you need a database expert on the team until too late in the project.
3. *Test yourself.* It may be hard to accept, but you may not know as much as you think you do. For the sake of this example, try explaining how a toilet or cell phone works. You use them all the time but will probably identify areas you don't fully comprehend. When you start a new project, try explaining all the steps and how they fit together. Make a note of the places where you get stuck.
4. *Be cautious.* You know and understand that you don't know everything. You also understand that there is a long list of things you know you don't know. It is important to remember that there are things you haven't realized you don't know. Use extra caution when you try something new, visit a new place, try a new activity, etc. There are risks and hazards you simply don't know to learn more about. There is a great deal of encouragement in this book for being courageous and bold. Don't forget this one caution.

Knowing what you don't know is a superpower. Because Philippe and his team know what they don't know and find help and guidance to fill their gaps, they are much safer during explorations, and the videos they produce are far more beautiful. You can do it, too!

Dr. NanaEfua Baidoo Afoh-Manin

Chapter 26: Laughter and Dancing - NanaEfua Baidoo Afoh-Manin

Devin: *Nana, what is your superpower?*

Nana: Definitely, my superpower is laughter and dancing. I think that it's just the honest–just getting–I say I laugh from the gut. My husband used to say you have such an infectious laugh because I think that's just the honest spirit of people, right? And just breaking down, everything seems so insurmountable. And so, you laugh about it. And then you get back down to the work of it.

And for me, also dancing helps me shake it off, get honest, get vulnerable, and I remember I always laugh about this. There was a guy; I don't know if you remember, he was a YouTube phenom because he went traveling around the world dancing in these smaller communities. I said, "I wish I could do that!" So that's definitely my superpower. And I can get people to get on the dance floor. So, watch out, Devin.

You can watch the full interview with Nana here: nana.s4g.biz.

NanaEfua Baidoo Afoh-Manin is included as an unequivocal intellectual and impact peer to anyone in this book. As you read this chapter about laughing and dancing, don't imagine a silly sophomore. Remember the emergency room doctor who saves lives every day and the public health expert who has devoted free time throughout the COVID-19 pandemic to serving her community.

Her larger-than-life, high energy, fueled by optimism and positivity, makes her truly powerful—no metaphor here. Nana BAM (she frequently abbreviates her last names that way) is a person you'd love to know. In a crisis, she's the one you need to know.

Three years ago, I caught up with her for Forbes when she and some of her MD friends launched a crowdfunding program called Shared Harvest Fund. It helps drive more people to serve nonprofits by helping to pay off their student loans. She shifted much of her energy during the pandemic to organizing community relief.

"I like to shake things up, and I have never met a challenge I didn't want to tackle. I have used my medical and public health training to serve communities in need all over the world from Rwanda to Haiti, and in disaster settings from Hurricane Katrina to the Ebola crisis," is how Nana introduced herself to me.

As we talked about her work and experience, she made a profound observation. At some level, I think she was talking about herself and her exuberant personality. But, more importantly, she was speaking to you. She said, "you can only be great at being you."

In this book, you've read and will continue to read about others' superpowers. But, sometimes, you'll think, "I can't do that." You might even think, "I can't be great if I can't do that." Don't go there! Her point is the opposite. You can't be great at being Bill Gates. You can only be great at being you. If you have the same talents, skills and abilities as Nana or anyone else in this book, you can be more like them. Wonderful! If not, you can always be great at being you. I'm confident you will find superpowers in this book that you share. So, bring them to the dance.

How to Develop Laughter and Dancing as a Superpower

"Wait," you may be thinking. "Laughter and dancing are not superpowers." I'm here to tell you they are. And they're equal to any in this book. Let's talk about how you can master them.

Laughter is how Nana puts problems in a better perspective. If you can laugh at a problem, it can't eat you. It can't hurt you. You are in control. Laughing at a challenge can give you the courage to face something you otherwise couldn't.

Dancing is Nana's way of energizing herself and her team. Picture her working an overnight shift in the emergency department at Kaiser Permanente in Los Angeles. It's 3:00 AM, and everyone is tired and cranky—the patients and the staff. Then, imagine her literally dancing into the room. Your first reaction could be like mine—wanting to hide. But, after seeing her broad smile and hearing her infectious laugh as she drags you and the rest of the team to their feet dancing, the mood of the room completely changes. Energy is restored. Priorities are reset. Lives are being saved.

Here are some tips to help you bring laughter and dancing to challenging situations.

1. *Use a crutch.* There is a saying in public speaking, "you only have to be funny if you want to be paid." Once, I attended a day-long seminar by a world-famous speaker. This guy was making a fortune. So, I was intrigued that he could not tell a joke to save his life. But he repeatedly got us laughing anyway. He put up slides of funny comics. YouTube has an infinite supply of funny videos to share with colleagues on your phone. If you can't tell a joke, share a cat video.
2. *Dance like nobody's watching.* Use Iggy Azalea for inspiration if need be. Then, when the situation demands it, forget yourself and dance. The point is not to be great or beautiful. If you dance like Elaine from "Seinfeld" (who famously danced awkwardly—that's being kind), remember your dance moves don't matter. The confidence, energy, and positivity you bring to a down moment can be a critical part of solving a problem.
3. *Be the producer.* When you can't lead the dance, think of yourself as the producer, and find someone like Nana to lead the dance. Then, be sure to join in to build the momentum. If you hang back, you'll give everyone else license to abstain.

You can be the one to lift the mood and bring the energy. Here's a final consideration: there are other ways to deliver positivity to a room exhausted by a challenge. Find your favorite way to encourage, uplift and inspire and use that even if it doesn't involve rap music.

Following this model, you can make laughter and dancing a superpower. Even if that isn't you, find your own way to lift spirits and bring positive energy when problems threaten to overwhelm you. You've got this!

Mari Kuraishi

Chapter 27: Learning - Mari Kuraishi

Devin: *Mari, what's your superpower?*

Mari: *I love to learn new things, and I like to think that other people in this organization are motivated to learn new things because I'm constantly sending out Slack messages, e-mail messages, you know, about, check out this new article. Did you see what so-and-so said? Think about the implications for this. I find all this work incredibly important, incredibly fascinating. The other thing that I'm incredibly grateful for is that this has been a job where I learn every day.*

You can watch the full interview with Mari here: mari.s4g.biz.

Mari Kuraishi co-founded and later led Global Giving, a nonprofit crowdfunding site for international development that could be the first crowdfunding site ever. She created it with Dennis Whittle (see Chapter 41) about a decade before Indiegogo or Kickstarter launched.

While at the World Bank, Mari learned that at the same time it was providing money to a few large institutions in each country, there were millions of people and small organizations working to solve problems. These folks needed money, too. She concluded that if they received the funds required, they could solve many of their own issues.

Years later, while networking, Mari met a person who responded to her introduction as a leader at Global Giving by saying, "Oh, I've heard of you guys. You guys work with the great unwashed."

"My jaw dropped," Mari says. "I mean, first, because the statement was outrageous, even back in 2001, right? But then I was like, 'Yes, damn it. We are the outfit that works for the great unwashed.'"

And work she has. Since its founding, Global Giving has raised over $500 million for international nonprofits serving people in the developing world. In 2020 alone, donations reached $100 million.

Mari is proud of the flexible culture she led at Global Giving. Having come from a large organization with many rules, she helped form a company governed by values instead. The company focuses on the mission and challenges employees not to complete tasks but to contribute meaningfully to accomplishing the primary goal to help people in the developing world.

Mari says she's not sure her ability and enthusiasm for learning have contributed directly to Global Giving's measurable impact on people around the world. As the objective arbiter I've appointed myself to be, I am sure. Her superpower has helped change the world for the better.

How to Develop Learning as a Superpower

You can become a better learner. If you take to it like Mari, it can become your superpower. To help me with this book, Mari agreed to a follow-up interview that you can watch here: mari2.s4g.biz.

Mari notes that it is vital to know yourself. She observed that she liked to develop a plan and stick to it. Events that derailed her plans irritated her. Over the years, she's learned to adapt and now celebrates the sorts of events that once annoyed her. She sees how even significant events that impose life-altering adjustments can be good things. She recognizes that she has found wonderful things at points in her life precisely because of a derailment.

Take time to get to know yourself. Mari says one of the vital things to understand about yourself and learning is that "people learn in different ways." You need to know what sort of learner you are.

Scientists haven't settled firmly on the number of discreet learning styles. One popular model is called VARK, an acronym for four learning styles.

- *Visual.* These learners (I think I'm in this group) learn by seeing things.
- *Auditory.* This group learns by hearing lessons.
- *Reading and writing.* Such students learn best by reading and writing about a subject.

- *Kinesthetic.* Some people learn by touching or by doing a task better than by other methods.

Most people learn best in one way, but that doesn't mean they only do it in that style. It is easy to find simplistic online assessments to help you assess your learning style. That may be an excellent place to start.

Mari's primary lesson about learning is profound. Rather than focus on learning facts, processes or skills, she talked about the need to learn about people. She said, "Every place and every person—even organizations—has a story that's unique."

The lesson from Mari is in how we get past the surface level familiarity with people to find deeper hidden realities. She uses the example of your reaction to a friend or colleague who says, "Oh, I didn't sleep well last night." What you say next will determine what you learn.

Imagine how different the response to each of the following reactions will be.

- "Well, did you drink coffee last night?"
- "Oh, I'm sorry to hear that; what was going on that made you not sleep well last night?"

From the second reaction question, you could learn something that matters. "You might discover something about that person that you had no idea about, even though you may have been working with that person for years," Mari says.

"Happy families are all alike; every unhappy family is unhappy in its own way," wrote Tolstoy as the opening line to Anna Karenina. Mari points out that learning to know people is about understanding Tolstoy's message and applying it in our interactions with others.

As you think about learning, you may see yourself in Mari. You may be capable of learning as a superpower. I'm convinced it can help you change the world. If it's not your superpower, it could at least make you happier.

"Anyone who is open to learning, and the change that comes from learning, might end up happier," Mari says.

Nicholas Kristof

Chapter 28: Choosing a Life Partner - Nicholas Kristof

Devin: I wonder, what is your superpower?

Nick: Well, I mean, look, I worked very, very hard. I've been incredibly blessed with a wife and partner, Sheryl WuDunn. If your family life is a mess, then that takes a personal and professional toll. I'm very lucky to be still in love with Sheryl. We maintained a professional and personal partnership that has certainly been a pillar of helping me with everything I've been able to achieve. The most important decision that young people make is not the company that they join or the career that they choose. It's the partner they choose for life. And I hit the jackpot there, too.

You can watch the full interview with Nick here: nick.s4g.biz.

Nicholas Kristof is a two-time Pulitzer Prize-winning columnist for the New York Times—and a role model for me and countless others. He's the co-author of *Half The Sky, A Path Appears* and *Tightrope*, each written with his wife, Sheryl WuDunn. In July of 2021, Nick took a leave of absence from the Times to consider running for Governor in Oregon.

Nick and Sheryl won a Pulitzer for their coverage of the Tiananmen Square massacre for the Times. Nick won his second for his coverage of the genocide in Darfur. Both Prizes recognized that they did their reporting at peril to their lives.

Nick is a towering figure in my life because he writes about the same sorts of things I do, just better. And he got there first. When I visited the Gates Foundation a few years ago, I discovered a museum-like welcome center that explains its work and mission. Included is what I can best describe as an homage to Nick for the influence his writing has had on the Foundation's work.

Think about the lives impacted by the Gates Foundation and consider what it means to have influenced its work in that way. If Nick's impact stopped there, it would be an abiding legacy. But it doesn't stop there. His reach and influence continue to grow.

Nick and Sheryl's books take an approach that has helped inspire a movement in their profession called "solutions journalism." The fundamental principle is that writers must thoughtfully and critically consider effective solutions rather than write only about a problem.

Half the Sky serves to do that for women worldwide, inspired by the Chinese tradition that women hold up half the sky. *Tightrope* looks primarily at disadvantaged communities in the United States, using Nick's childhood classmates in Yamhill, Oregon as a lens. About a quarter of the kids he rode the bus to school with have died "deaths of despair," he says.

Three times during our conversation, Nick repeated the aphorism, "Talent is universal. Opportunity is not." He reiterated this to make the point that despite having worked hard and having been blessed with talent, he was given opportunities others did not receive. He notes that the admissions panel at Harvard included someone from rural Oregon, like him, who thought (correctly) that Nick would add value to the class. *Tightrope* is about the structural inequities that disadvantage low-income communities and people of color and how to repair those structures to serve everyone better.

It takes only a cursory glance at Nick's story to appreciate the veracity and significance of his observation that Sheryl WuDunn is his superpower. Sheryl, however, is not a skill you can learn. She is not replicable. You cannot have her as your life partner—nor superpower. That said, you can choose a life partner and maintain the sort of relationship Nick and Sheryl have.

How to Develop Choosing a Life Partner as a Superpower

Nick and Sheryl are partners. That's a model for finding and building a lifelong relationship that could serve you as a superpower.

There are three things to consider.

1. *Choose to partner.* "The most important decision that young people make is not the company that they join or the career that they choose. It's the partner they choose for life," Nick said. Implicit in that statement is the advice to choose to find a partner. Are there exceptions that make sense? Yes. That said, the trend toward going it alone in life conflicts with his experience and counsel. He feels—and the evidence supports him—that he and Sheryl have accomplished more together than they could have separately.

2. *Find a partner.* Looking for a life partner isn't easy for many people. But, of course, modernity provides tools for pairing that folks like Nick and Sheryl didn't have. My son and his fiance, who connected via an app, are a case in point I celebrate; they are great individuals who comprise a great pair. Based on my own experience, I would encourage you to use your volunteer work as a complementary path to your favorite app. As someone working to change the world, a great way to find a soul mate would be to volunteer regularly for the causes you care about to find like-minded life partner candidates.

3. *Invest in the relationship.* Nick and Sheryl model a relationship of equals. Make that a goal. In my own experience, I've seen three approaches to coupling. A level one relationship is built on the false premise that your partner is responsible for your happiness. A level two pairing is based on a more mature understanding that you remain independent human beings accountable for your own self-actualization. Finally, a level three connection occurs when you and your partner both seek to make your partner happy as the top priority.

As you can see, level one relationships are doomed. My experience is that level two couples sometimes end because people evolve on separate paths. Level three relationships endure.

Choosing a fantastic life partner and building on that foundation can make a real difference in your ability to impact the world positively. Your partner can become your superpower in much the same way Sheryl is Nick's.

Dr. Briana DeCuit

Chapter 29: Multitasking - Briana DeCuir

Devin: *Briana, what is your superpower?*

Briana: *I would have to say, as a pretty busy emergency physician and single mother now—also now founder of this wonderful organization—I would have to say multitasking. I think I would say that about most mothers and fathers and people who have families. Even if you don't, everyone has to learn to multitask because getting into the idea of being able to do everything all at once is feasible but not often something that people can do. So, I think I've mastered that fairly well.*

You can watch the full interview with Briana here: briana.s4g.biz.

Dr. Briana DeCuir is an emergency physician and co-founder of Shared Harvest Fund, along with her friend Dr. NanaEfua Baidoo Afoh-Manin, profiled in Chapter 26. Briana brings the same passion for the work, sacrificing her valuable time to launch and run the fund to help people do more good in the world and pay down their student loans.

Given their business partnership, it isn't necessary to revisit the inspirational work of the Shared Harvest Fund. If you're reading chapters out of order, however, let me encourage you now to read Chapter 26 for context.

Like Nana, Briana is well educated, having earned her undergraduate and MD degrees at the University of Rochester and then completing her residency at the University of Chicago.

During our conversation, I asked Briana for the most important lesson she'd learned from her experience as a doctor and social entrepreneur. Her response: resilience.

Briana explains, "I think the most important lesson that I've learned is that you have to be resilient and not give up." She and Nana both spent over ten years in training and education to become physicians. That alone makes her an expert on resilience.

She ties this to investing time and energy in volunteerism for causes and organizations that you supported that way early in your career or as a student. While success requires sacrifice, she notes that sacrificing volunteerism could be bad for your health.

"There was a recent survey that was done, and over 74 percent of people actually are now getting to the point of having depression and anxiety and physical symptoms regarding just having student loan debt," she says. "So, I think it's important to know that you can be resilient, that there are options that are out there that help improve the way you look at yourself in the world and what impact you feel like you're making on the world, and volunteering does that for everyone."

As you think about folding volunteerism into your busy life to improve your health and become more resilient, you may find yourself thinking about how to model her superpower of multitasking.

How to Develop Multitasking as a Superpower

Briana highlights the three roles that compete for her time and attention: single mother, social entrepreneur and emergency physician. She attributes her success to multitasking.

Would you like to learn how to do that better? Dr. Ron Knaus explains that you can, reiterating that multitasking is a learned skill.[10] Those who don't master it are more likely to feel stress and anxiety, especially at work.

He offers five tips to help you multitask.

1. *Practice.* The simple act of deliberate practice will help you make progress in multitasking. Start with a few familiar tasks and slowly add more complex tasks going forward.

---

[10] Dr. Ron Knaus, American Management Association, "Secrets of Multitasking: Slow Down to Speed Up," January 24, 2019, https://www.amanet.org/articles/secrets-of-multitasking-slow-down-to-speed-up/.

2. *Set priorities.* Switching from task to task uses up a bit of your mental energy. The more you switch, the more bandwidth you use in alternating among functions. By prioritizing and focusing for a time on one task, you're more able to make progress, using less energy for managing all the open tabs on your brain's browser.

3. *Use tools.* It's not cheating to write things down. When you store information outside of your brain, it will forget it, allowing you to focus your remaining capacity on more important things. You can use software, online tools or your phone to help you keep track of your to-do list, procedural checklists and data sets.

4. *Rest by focusing.* Because focusing on a single task is less stressful on your brain, you can recharge your capacity for multitasking by concentrating for a while on a single job. Your brain will thank you, and you'll get more done.

5. *Take a break.* You likely know that when you stop for a grown-up recess, you relax and feel better. What you may not fully appreciate is that you're probably able to get more done in the day if you take a couple of breaks and stop for lunch. When you tire, you are less productive.

You can be like Briana. You can learn to multitask. Even if you don't make it your superpower, working to increase your productivity can also help you optimize your impact.

Ibrahim AlHusseini

Sandra Rey

Chapter 30: Naivete - Ibrahim AlHusseini and Sandra Rey

Ibrahim AlHusseini, CEO and Founder, FullCycle

Devin: *What is your superpower, Ibrahim?*

Ibrahim: *My superpower is being naive enough to believe that anything I was building was going to succeed.*

You can watch the full interview with Ibrahim here: ibrahim.s4g.biz.

Sandra Rey, CEO and Founder, Glowee

Devin: *Sandra, what is your superpower?*

Sandra: *My superpower is that I don't have superpowers. I'm just realizing that right now. But I think my superpower is to think that I can have superpowers. Yeah, until I realized that I don't. But I'm a bit naive. And I think that helps a lot. That's kind of my superpower.*

You can watch the full interview with Sandra here: sandra.s4g.biz.

Ibrahim AlHusseini and Sandra Rey are remarkably different people doing strikingly disparate things to address climate change but share a common superpower: naivete.

Ibrahim, CEO and founder of the investment firm FullCycle, is working to increase funding for scalable climate solutions. For instance, the firm invested in Synova, which converts trash, including plastic, into energy at a price that works in the developing world, where such solutions are often out of financial reach. FullCycle also invested in Sustainitech, which is building indoor farms that capture carbon rather than emit it. The latter investment has the potential to address food supply issues even while it addresses climate change.

Having faced and overcome challenges helped Ibrahim develop a positive mindset. As an immigrant child of Palestinian refugees, Ibrahim recognizes that it is remarkable that his outlook is optimistic. He sees climate change not only as a problem that must be solved but also as an opportunity.

Sandra began working on her company, Glowee, as a design student in France. She entered a design competition with the theme "biology." Employing a concept known as biomimicry, she developed a plan to harness bioluminescence as a light source for humans.

She confesses that her early efforts yielded such low light, it took her ten or 15 minutes in total darkness to see it. Over time, she and her team were able to increase the brightness by 200 fold.

Seven years later, she has raised millions of dollars and is developing a range of lighting products that require no electricity. While none are bright enough to read by, they can provide beautiful aesthetic and mood lighting indoors and out.

The light comes from sea bacteria with natural bioluminescence. By depriving them of oxygen, the bacteria become dormant, and the light goes out. Restore the oxygen, and it returns, providing a sort of on-off switch.

Lighting without electricity has the potential to make a difference in a global effort to reverse climate change.

Sandra used her naivete to try something that had never been done before. She's now proven that it has commercial and positive environmental potential. Ibrahim used his naivete to scale up his investment firm to make a measurable difference in an almost immeasurably large problem. You may be able to use your remaining naivete for good, too.

How to Develop Naivete as a Superpower

Of course, it is unfair and perhaps impolite to describe either Sandra or Ibrahim as naive. Still, they described it as their superpower. How could that be?

Sometimes, what you don't know allows you to try something you wouldn't try if you knew better. You might try a solution to a problem that is so odd that experts would reject it—and it just might work. Naively, you could try to do something that you wouldn't dare tackle if you had more experience. Not knowing it's an uphill battle allows you to launch, becoming so committed you could go on to finish successfully.

Should you nurture your naivete? That would mean choosing to remain intentionally ignorant. Ultimately, Sandra succeeded in developing beautiful lighting not because she was still naive about the science of bioluminescence but because she wasn't. Ibrahim launched an effort that is extraordinarily difficult for most people but succeeded. His launch was guided in part by naivete. Successfully putting together offering documents, raising tens of millions of dollars and investing it in high-impact companies required a broad and deep set of skills, which he has now honed.

When you have an idea for impact, the way to leverage your naivete is to move quickly. Learn as you go. In the entrepreneurial world, aspiring startup leaders are encouraged to test a "minimum viable product" or MVP. You can do the same in the impact arena.

Look for a way to create a simple version of your solution as affordably as possible and build it. Think of Sandra sitting in the dark staring at a jar that might be glowing just a bit. Once proven, the world begins to change.

The next step is to get your target users testing your MVP to see if they like it enough to use it. Whether you are thinking about a next-generation clean cookstove for low-income families or a better battery for electric vehicles, get your MVP in front of potential customers to see what they think.

Along the way, you'll need to learn much more than you know now—and you will gain that knowledge. If you learn quickly that your idea is fundamentally flawed, you've done so fast, and you can move on. But you may find that your idea is good and with more knowledge you can make it even better.

You will never have more naivete than you have right now. Don't squander it. It just might be your superpower.

Kristin Nimsger

Chapter 31: Never Being Satisfied - Kristin Nimsger

Devin: *Kris, what is your superpower?*

Kristin: *My superpower? So, I think everything's always a double-edged sword, right? But I think my superpower probably is never being satisfied. Never, never, never being satisfied. Personally, with the team, with the business, with my chess game, with my lap times in the car, just never being satisfied. I think that while that might plague me and plague my sleep at times, I think it probably serves me well as well.*

You can watch the full interview with Kristin here: kris.s4g.biz.

When we connected, Kristin Nimsger was the CEO of Social Solutions, a tech company specializing in case management software for nonprofits and public entities. She is also one of the most interesting people I've ever had on the podcast. Today, she is an operating partner at the private equity firm Thoma Bravo.

A relatively young mother and CEO are two roles that should go together more often than they do and shouldn't be so hard for me to comprehend. Being raised in a place and time where that was almost unheard of shouldn't make it so difficult for me to understand.

However, my brain almost broke when she told me she is also an avid racecar driver. That's how she releases tension, by driving more than 100 miles per hour around a 1.8 mile, 12-turn track in the BMW M4 she also takes to work. So, can we agree that she is not a typical young mother?

One of the things that nonprofits use Social Solutions software for is measuring impact. Kristin's all about that. She loved leading a growing tech company, especially one that drives positive social impact with every sale.

"No one likes to win more than I do," she told me. She also likes "helping nonprofits win." The solutions she sold help nonprofits care for people, track results, raise more money and improve outcomes.

She and I had the chance to talk when former Microsoft CEO Steve Ballmer committed to invest $59 million into the 18-year-old company to help it accelerate growth. As we chatted, she admitted that this likely represented the greatest accomplishment of her career to that time.

As you consider this highly competitive, data-focused leader, it isn't surprising that her superpower is never being satisfied. Don't be intimidated. You can emulate that energy to help you do more good, too.

How to Develop Never Being Satisfied as a Superpower

Kristin is a powerhouse. She gets crucial things done. She makes a difference. She is successful. Never being satisfied is truly her superpower. You can be like her.

One way to think about this is how to avoid being mediocre, rising above the average and standing out. Here are some tips to help you do just that.

1. *Measure performance.* You can't improve if you don't set objective standards to calibrate to determine how you, your team, or your operation perform. It is unfair to you and anyone else you measure to use anything other than an objective standard. Caution: make sure you measure the right things. The old axiom, what gets measured gets done still holds. The corollary is that what doesn't get measured doesn't get done.
2. *Set SMART goals.* Remember the acronym SMART when setting your goals: Specific, Measurable, Attainable, Relevant and Time-bound. You may want to build a goal structure that includes small, tactical short-term goals that support and lead to accomplishing long-term, strategic goals.
3. *Compare appropriately.* In most cases, simply comparing your current measurable performance to your past measurable performance is helpful. For example, does it help you to look at your 5k run time next to the world record? Unless you are an elite-level athlete, it probably doesn't. But, on the other hand, comparing

your average running pace this year to last year can be an excellent gauge of your overall training.

4. *Eliminate excuses.* In the professional speaker community, there is a remarkable work ethic. Every successful speaker I know has a story about giving a speech when most people would cancel. When flights were canceled, they drove through the night to get to the event and deliver a speech. They received tragic news, walked on stage and gave their standard comedy-filled inspiration. They know if they don't show up, they don't get paid. Check your excuses. When others are counting on you, are you showing up?

5. *Cut distractions.* Never in the history of the world have there been so many distractions. In this day and age of Slack, email, instant messaging, video calls and all the rest, it is difficult even to define what a distraction is. So when required, turn everything off but the top priority and focus on that. If you can, make that a daily habit for a few hours.

6. *Connect to passion.* Constantly working to improve your performance can be challenging. To motivate you, connect the process of improvement to your passion. If you can't make the connection, ask yourself if you're focusing on the proper measurement (see the caution in Item 1.)

7. *Be patient.* Give yourself and others time to make measurable progress, achieve goals and generally play at the expected level. If you label early efforts a failure, progress is more likely to stop than accelerate.

If you follow these steps, you can not only improve your performance but also develop a habit of making perpetual progress. You can add a new superpower: never being satisfied.

Piyush Jain

Chapter 32: Perspective - Piyush Jain

Devin: *Piyush, what's your superpower?*

Piyush: *I think I've been fairly lucky to be able to focus on the micro details as well as being able to not lose out on the big picture in terms of what we are trying to achieve. And that's a delicate balance that's very important for any leader in any organization. And I feel that that has helped me contribute a lot towards this particular mission.*

You can watch the full interview with Piyush here: piyush.s4g.biz.

Piyush Jain is the co-founder, with his wife Khushboo (see Chapter 57), of Impact Guru, a crowdfunding site similar to GoFundMe operating in India. Perhaps because its healthcare system isn't as developed as in some more prosperous countries and many people lack access to private health insurance, the site is a lifeline for survival for many Indians.

Piyush has an impressive résumé. Educated at the University of Pennsylvania's Wharton School and Harvard's Kennedy School, he has experience in both the private and public sector, including investment banking experience with JP Morgan.

Perhaps his first look at social entrepreneurship was during his graduate studies at Harvard, where he did his capstone project on corporate social responsibility and crowdfunding.

119

Since its founding in 2014, more than 20,000 patients have raised money for care on Impact Guru—many of them raising money that represented the difference between life and death. The relevance of the effort came into stark focus during the pandemic as it became clear that most Indians could not afford the healthcare they needed.

During the pandemic, Piyush and Khushboo made a generous decision to waive platform fees on ImpactGuru, making it essentially free to raise money on the platform. As a result, the website is replete with stories of people who successfully raised money to save or extend the life of a loved one.

Eric Pereira, the father of Ezekiel, said, "Watching my child fight hard to survive blood cancer was the most heartbreaking thing for us. I couldn't afford his chemo, and that's when I set up a fundraiser on ImpactGuru.com. Today, my son receives regular chemotherapy sessions. Thanks for the generosity of so many donors."

The ability to be mindful of Ezekiel when he simultaneously sees the healthcare crisis facing the country—in fact, the entire world—is how Piyush manifests his superpower, what I call perspective. He can see the forest without losing sight of one tree.

You can learn to do the same.

How to Develop Perspective as a Superpower

Piyush notes correctly that being able to focus at once on the micro-details of a situation while maintaining the clarity to see the big picture is a powerful leadership skill. Furthermore, he's right that this mindset is unusual. In my experience, people tend to focus on one or the other.

Mother Teresa built a large global organization, the Missionaries of Charity, that operated in 133 countries around the world. She also famously said, "Never worry about numbers. Help one person at a time and always start with the person nearest you." Piyush may not think of it this way, but his ability to focus on details without losing sight of the bigger context emulates Mother Teresa.

Here are some tips to help you develop the superpower perspective to see details and their context at once.

First, split your time. If you want to be engaged in details and on the big picture, you've got to allocate some of your time to work that brings each of those angles into view. Spend some time on tasks like studying a high-level dashboard of data that can give you a clear image of the whole project, company or operations. Talk to other people in the organization with broad perspectives to hear about what they're seeing.

When working to solve global problems like climate, poverty and health, you likely need to get out of your office and into the field where you can see and interact with the people most acutely impacted by the problem you are working to solve. But, unfortunately, that vantage point may not come cheap or easy. So, you'll need to make time for these activities that will expose you to the details.

There are also operational details that are likely important. Some of them you can't solve alone. However, your engagement with a customer service representative, software coder or web designer can both inform you about the realities of work in your operation and give you a chance to help solve problems your perspective addresses uniquely.

Second, take breaks. As you begin enhancing your view of either the big picture or the details, the issues you find will pull you into that work. Your bias will shift toward the angle you're currently working. Regardless of which perspective you're working to build, you need to step back, pause, and reflect from time to time. Put your new lens on to look at your former view. Think about how the added information enlightens, enhances or changes your conclusions.

Taking a break will help you develop perspective like photographers develop film into photos in a dark room. Far from the action, in solitude, the photographer transfers the clear image from the film and enlarges it on paper. Make time to put your balanced views into a final, crisp perspective.

You may not feel you have access to this balanced perspective or the ability to make it a superpower. That's fair. You are likely able to seek additional information that will better inform you and help you be more successful at doing good. If you are in a position to gather a full range of views, perspective truly can become a superpower.

Suchita Guntakatta

Chapter 33: Problem Solving - Suchita Guntakatta

Devin: *Now, what's your superpower?*

Suchita: *Probably a problem solver. I really enjoy trying to figure out how to fix a particular issue or problem by looking at and understanding all angles, perspectives, options, solutions, both collectively and as an individual. I really enjoy that because you learn so much in that process. So I'd say problem-solving.*

You can watch the full interview with Suchita here: suchita.s4g.biz.

Suchita Guntakatta is the deputy director of strategy, planning and management for polio eradication at the Bill & Melinda Gates Foundation, where she has worked for over a dozen years.

As a finance guy myself, I'm excited to see business acumen like Suchita's put to work to benefit a global health initiative such as polio eradication. Just since she joined the team, she has seen polio eradicated from India—where some worried it might be the most challenging—and from the entire continent of Africa.

A generation ago, in the United States, most adults could identify someone they knew who had survived polio. Some survivors walk with a limp. Others use wheelchairs. A few require ventilators to help them breathe. And not everyone who contracted polio survived.

In 1952, for instance, 58,000 people, primarily children, caught polio. About 3,000 died. The rest suffered permanent disabilities. Poorly understood until decades later, polio survivors face a second round of challenges later in life. Its lasting impact can debilitate people who were able to walk for decades.

Today, most adults in the United States don't know anyone who survived polio. The vaccine was introduced in 1956 and was widely available beginning in 1957. The last case of polio in the United States occurred in 1979, just 22 years later. Most survivors here are well over 60 years old, and it has been a long time since kids had classmates who were affected.

By the mid-1980s, however, polio continued to rage worldwide, outside of the wealthiest nations. There were about 350,000 cases per year then. Then, with support from the U.S. Centers for Disease Control, Rotary International launched the effort to eradicate polio. UNICEF and the World Health Organization joined the partnership known as the Global Polio Eradication Initiative. Critically, the Gates Foundation joined the team early in this century, becoming the largest funding source for the Initiative.

The Gates Foundation has now donated about $4 billion to fight polio. As a senior member of the Foundation's team, Suchita leverages her business skills, honed at the giant consulting firm Accenture.

She sees herself as a problem solver. I see polio as a problem, so I'm grateful to see her working to solve it. With polio endemic in only two countries, the operation is embedded with a series of problems, from conflicts in Afghanistan to reluctant parents in Pakistan. She plays a critical role in closing the book on a disease that has plagued humans for millennia.

You can learn to be a problem solver, too.

How to Develop Problem-Solving as a Superpower

While I suspect Suchita doesn't deliberately use the problem-solving method below, I'd bet she recognizes the pattern in her polio eradication work.

In 1945, the mathematician George Polya wrote the bestselling book *How to Solve it*. The model he set out is a guide to solving math problems. However, it's an equally brilliant approach for challenges we may not see, at least initially, as math questions. Here are the four basic steps.

1. *Understand the problem.* You know you can't solve a problem you don't comprehend adequately. Sometimes, in real life, as opposed to a math quiz, understanding the problem is the problem. Spend as much time as possible learning about the issue. Think about new ways to diagram or visualize the problem.

2. *Devise a plan.* Once you have a grasp of the problem, devise a plan to solve it. The bigger the problem, the more detailed the solution needs to be. Incorporate the diagrams or visualizations you conceived in the first step to help you set up a better solution. Put the plan to paper.

3. *Carry out the plan.* Sometimes, implementing the plan will be easier than designing it. Whether that is the case or not, at some point, you have to attempt a solution.

4. *Review the outcome.* This final step could be the most important. You won't usually solve problems entirely on the first attempt. Sometimes, you may cause new problems with your intervention. Only a thoughtful, careful review can determine whether your solution is complete and what unintended consequences may have arisen. Don't brush this off.

Start your practice at problem-solving with small, simple ones. Follow these steps. Repeat the steps for more significant challenges until you've made problem-solving a Suchita-level superpower

Steve Stirling by Jensen Nemec

Chapter 34: Purpose - Steve Stirling

Devin: *So, Steve, what is your superpower?*

Steve: *I believe that I have a purpose in life and that for me, it's for my faith, because and for me, it's like I wonder why did I get polio? Why did I get abandoned? Why did kids make fun of me? I mean, it was tough. You know, it's challenging. And I'm thankful to be in the US because it's lots easier, but it's still challenging to put on my leg braces, walk, you fall, you get up. But I believe there's a—I have purpose in life, and it says that we are God's workmanship created in Jesus to do good works. So, for me, I have purpose. It's not a waste that I had polio. It's not for just—you know what, it's tough, and you've got to deal with it. For me to use that to help other people and to encourage other people, that's what drives me. And for me, it's not like work because I'm really trying to help people encourage them to say, hey, look, you can do it. If I can do it, you can do it. Hopefully, I can be an encouragement to other people.*

You can watch the full interview with Steve here: stirling.s4g.biz.

Steve Stirling is the CEO of MAP International and author of the inspiring memoir *The Crutch of Success*, which is about being abandoned by his parents, growing up with polio, becoming a successful contributor to society and the role of faith in his life. Educated at Cornell with an MBA from Northwestern University, he spent the first two decades of his career in the pharmaceutical industry. Later, Steve spent five years at the large NGO World Vision.

MAP International accepts donations of urgently needed, expensive medicine directly from drug companies. It distributes them worldwide, especially in Latin America, to people who cannot afford to buy the meds they need.

Due to his experience in both the pharmaceutical industry and the NGO world, Steve was recruited to lead MAP International in 2014.

Ray Knighton founded MAP International seemingly by accident. Some would argue providence lent a hand. In the 1940s, he repeatedly heard about Christian missionaries in faraway places unable to treat patients with simple problems because of a lack of drugs. He frequently mentioned this to people.

One day, a representative of a drug company called Ray to say, "We've shipped 11 tons of medicine to your office." Unprepared, he scrambled to organize the distribution of the massive donation and MAP International was born.

Today, Steve is the remarkable leader of that organization. Disabled by polio and abandoned by his birth parents, he is at peace with those challenges as they prepared him for a divine purpose, serving others. To him, the experience is poetic. He walks with braces on his legs using crutches today because a vaccine, available in the United States when he contracted the disease in 1957, was not given to him in South Korea. So, he knows firsthand and is reminded constantly of the importance of the work he leads, delivering desperately needed drugs to people who cannot afford to buy them.

He has a sense of divine purpose that serves as his superpower. You, too, can make purpose your superpower, even if you don't share Steve's Christian faith.

How to Develop Purpose as a Superpower

Like Steve, almost everyone profiled in this book feels a sense of purpose. He sees divine providence calling him to his. Others arrive at theirs by choice. If you are devout like Steve, you may already have a clear sense of your life's mission. Otherwise, you can consider the following ideas to help you find or choose your purpose.

Each of the following can help you frame the central theme of your life. Consider writing down your thoughts about each of these four topics in a two by two matrix or table to help you see and reflect upon your thoughts.

1. *Skills and talents.* You have a broad set of skills and talents. Some you learned in school and others perhaps for pleasure. For example, you likely learned to write and do math in school. You may have learned to play the drums or sing for fun. Now, those or other skills and talents you've developed are accessible to serve a life-defining purpose. In the upper left-hand quadrant, write down your talents, the things you do well, and put a star next to the ones you enjoy the most.

2. *Life circumstances.* Like Steve, your life has a variety of circumstances, some of which may not be positive. This exercise is just for you, so feel free to note everything that makes your life interesting. Steve is a polio survivor born in South Korea adopted by parents in the United States. Those factors have influenced who he is and his sense of purpose. So what are the historical and present situations that help define you? Write them down in the lower left-hand quadrant.

3. *Interests.* In the top, right-hand quadrant of your matrix, write down the things that interest you. It will be helpful to be honest with yourself. Think about the books you read, the movies and television you enjoy, the places you go on vacation and where you spend your money. Your charitable donations are entirely voluntary. Be sure to consider whether they correspond to your interests. Would you rather go to the park or the theater? Camping or stay in a hotel? Golf or a hike in the woods? Skiing or surfing?

4. *Passions.* This exercise could be challenging. If it would be safer for you to skip this quadrant to avoid painful triggers, or if you need someone to talk this through with you, be sure to take care of yourself. If and when you're ready, write down the things that make you angry or sad. Think about the times you got so mad you yelled at someone, broke something or hurt your hand, smacking it against the wall—or worse. Next, think about what triggered real tears—a painful sadness that made you feel desperate to either be alone or find a loved one for a hug. Now, in the final quadrant, write down the triggers that upset you. These are your real passions.

Once you've done the exercise, set it aside for a few hours. During this time, allow yourself to think about what you've missed or connect your interests to your passions. You may reflect on how your life circumstances influence your skills, interests and especially passions. Do this without structure.

Then, after a time away, come back to your matrix. Add the things you remembered. Look for the patterns that can guide your sense of mission. What do you see? With some reflection and focus, you may see something as powerful as Steve's seeing how his lack of a childhood vaccine motivates his life's work in the pharmaceutical and nonprofit space and provides a sense of purpose.

When you settle on a sense of purpose, write it down. Post it on the wall. Let it inspire your work—and your play—every day. Let it become your superpower.

Margret Trilli

Chapter 35: Strategy Development and Implementation - Margret Trilli

Devin: *What is your superpower, Margret?*

Margret: *One of my core values is being modest and humble. So, the way your question is framed is difficult for me. That said, I have been told by colleagues that I am a visionary and strategic leader.*

But I also really enjoy the execution. My strategies tend to always incorporate what's feasible, and they always extend through execution. I enjoy making the strategy come alive. I've spent times in my career where I was doing only one or only the other. And what surprised me is that when I was the head of strategy for an organization, I missed the execution. Not a lot of people like both. I do.

You can watch the full interview with Margret here: margret.s4g.biz.

Margret Trilli, the CEO of ImpactAssets, has helped accelerate the growth of the nonprofit impact investment company since she joined in the fall of 2018, tripling the assets. She has also led the dramatic expansion of giving.

During the COVID-19 pandemic, grants reached $200 million. At the same time, the organization made impact investments of the same scale, meaning that ImpactAssets deployed a total of $400 million for good during the crisis.

One example of an investment made by ImpactAssets was a $12 million fund created for microloans for smallholder farmers and entrepreneurs. The program ultimately made $63 million in loans to almost 1 million individuals by revolving the capital as borrowers repaid their loans. The funds were effectively recycled more than five times.

That $12 million fund is a powerful example of the difference made by the $1.5 billion Margret manages at ImpactAssets. It drives change for good and provides investors with a financial return.

Margret sees how her ability to develop strategy and execute the implementation successfully helps her drive more good. She can now create strategies that the organization can implement readily, moving quickly from ideation to impact.

She started her career on the execution side and loved it. She can see how to make things work considering the constraints, challenges and issues that her colleagues raise and addressing them.

You can learn to do the same.

How to Develop Strategy Development and Implementation as a Superpower

Margret joined me for a follow-up interview to discuss how you can learn to emulate her, making strategy development and implementation your superpower. You can watch that second interview here: margret2.s4g.biz.

She points out that many books are available to help you learn to think more strategically and execute more effectively. She encourages aspiring leaders to look for opportunities to work on both sides, spending time developing strength in both disciplines.

She offers additional insights to help people on each side to develop a greater understanding of the other side.

Those working on the strategy side, such as people who do or have done management consulting with a mandate to develop strategic plans, can develop execution chops using skills they already have. If you're in this group, look at how you can break down a strategy that may start with a big, hairy audacious goal (BHAG from Jim Collins' *Good to Great*) into smaller chunks.

As you work down into the details, more of what you'll need to address is operational. The more you think about the operational nuances, the better you'll execute on implementation when you have that opportunity.

She adds that it is vital for folks on the strategic side to respect the role of people doing the implementation. Their functions are critical. You may be tempted to scoff at the part of the corporate attorney, but by considering their concerns early in the process, you can accelerate and improve implementation. This is true across the organization. Consider as many of the functional issues as early in the process as possible.

On the other side, folks doing the crucial work of the company day in and day out may feel a desire for more strategic opportunities. Margret notes that everyone has opportunities to build those strategic muscles.

First, recognize that you are likely already doing some strategic work. Anytime you are revising a process or planning an event, you are strategic. By looking for ways to achieve something new or improve outcomes, you're thinking about how inputs lead to results. That's strategy.

Second, she says you can build your capacity to be strategic by intentionally using your growing strategic power to improve further the work you manage. By involving other people in your strategic initiatives, you build on your capacity.

Ultimately, whether you are coming from the strategic or operational side of the organization, you can strengthen your other abilities to become effective on both. Not everyone will achieve the mastery that Margret has. But by improving your ability to understand and do work across the strategy-implementation spectrum, you gain more capacity for having impact.

Gunnar Lovelace

Chapter 36: Uniqueness - Gunnar Lovelace

Devin: Gunnar, what is your superpower?

Gunnar: I very much use my business endeavors as a way to also just kind of constantly improve myself. I'm constantly humbled by the mistakes that I made in the midst of successes that I've been blessed with. I spent so much of my childhood kind of covering up from the fact that I came from a hippie commune, and I have a weird name, and I have a very, kind of weird upbringing. Increasingly, I've come to realize that something I have uniquely to offer is all of the uniqueness of that and really embracing that and embracing the idea that we are incredibly powerful when our hearts and our minds are aligned.

You can watch the full interview with Gunnar here: gunnar.s4g.biz.

"Growing up really poor, I saw money from very early on as a way to take care of people that I love and do good," said Gunnar Lovelace, founder of the organic online grocer Thrive Market and the newer Good Money.

Gunnar's remarkable success as a serial entrepreneur (Thrive Market and Good Money are just two of many startups he's launched) is inspiring because he is an immigrant who grew up in an intentional community he frequently refers to as a "hippie commune."

His mother, Adriana Goddard, is considered a dissident in her native Argentina. She fled in the 70s at a time when tens of thousands of people like her just disappeared. In the early 1980s, I spent two years in Argentina. I remember seeing the grandmothers maintaining a vigil protest in the center of Buenos Aires looking for their adult children (perhaps murdered) and grandchildren (possibly stolen).

Channeling his childhood desire to use money for good, Gunnar is working to scale Good Money, a banking app owned significantly by the customers, which will offer no-fee transactions and relatively generous interest on deposits. And, of paramount import to him, Good Money won't use customers' deposits to fund private prisons or fossil fuel development.

Gunnar notes that too many banks today prey on consumers by, for instance, deducting the value of larger checks before smaller ones to increase the number of overdraft fees they can assess. Then, when customers can't pay, they are blackballed in banking and forced into an even more predatory payday lending and check cashing economy.

Good Money won't charge overdraft fees, Gunnar pledges. Furthermore, by effectively setting up the financial institution as a co-op, he plans to ensure that all customers receive ownership. This means that the customers will share in the profits.

Additionally, Gunnar is devoting a portion of the profits to social impact through both philanthropic giving and impact investing—financially backing for-profit projects that do good. Suffice it to say, Good Money is not your typical bank.

A financial business as different as Good Money could only come from someone who recognizes his unique perspective and experience as his superpower. You are unique, too. You can make it one of your superpowers.

How to Develop Uniqueness as a Superpower

Gunnar celebrates the experience and perspective he has that are unusual. He has become proud of his uniqueness. Not being the same as others is not a handicap in any way. It is his superpower. Uniqueness can be one of your superpowers, too.

First, use the following checklist to help you identify your uniqueness. Grab a sheet of paper and scrawl answers or just words that come to mind as you go through this list.

1. Where were you born? How does the place you live compare to your birthplace?
2. What is interesting about your childhood?
3. How does your education influence your perspective?
4. Where have you traveled? How much do you travel?

5. What is your family situation?
6. How many jobs have you had? Which was your favorite?
7. Describe your faith. How has it changed over your lifetime?
8. What music, movies and books do you enjoy as entertainment?
9. What are the sources of information you rely on today?
10. Who follows your example, listens to your thoughts or does what you say?

Now, look at the mess you've made on your sheet of paper. Can you imagine that anyone has an identical sheet? Of course not! Now, with a bit more discipline and care, write three sentences that explain your uniqueness.

Having established that you are genuinely unique, you need to believe in yourself. You need the self-confidence necessary to use your authentic, unusual and custom-built lens for seeing the world to change it in ways that will make it better.

Psychologists suggest the following to help you gain self-confidence.[11]

1. *Tally your success.* Write down all the things you've done successfully. Consider every aspect of your life. You've done a lot. Think of your professional, educational, social, service, community, faith-based and just-for-fun victories. Write them all down.
2. *List strengths and weaknesses.* Take a few minutes to write down your strengths and weaknesses with one constraint: list at least two strengths for every weakness. Be sure to include all the superpowers described in this book (flip to the table of contents) you have already mastered.
3. *Stop negative self-talk.* Start monitoring your self-talk, including your thoughts. When you start getting down on yourself, stop it! Consciously choose to think positive thoughts instead. Whatever goes wrong, reassure yourself the way you would a friend.
4. *Pick new superpowers.* Pick a few superpowers from this book that you haven't mastered but hope to develop. Write down your plan based on the guidance provided in the book for adding them.
5. *Celebrate progress.* Mark your progress as you make progress toward new superpowers. Celebrate it.

As you develop your superpowers (your ability to change the world for good), your self-confidence will grow. Your ability to manifest your unique

---

[11] February 18, 2021, Courtney E. Ackerman, Psychology Today, "12 Tips For Building Self-Confidence and Self-Belief," https://positivepsychology.com/self-confidence-self-belief/.

perspective will begin to look like Gunnar's. Ultimately, your uniqueness can become your most powerful tool for good.

Part 3: Networking

Networking, the practice of strategically building relationships with people has been a proven tactic for business success for more than a generation. Remember the refrain "it's not what you know, it's who you know." In Part 3, you'll read about people who are using their networking superpowers for good.

Pia Wilson-Body

Suzanne DiBianca

Chapter 37: Connecting - Pia Wilson-Body and Suzanne DiBianca

Pia Wilson-Body, President, Intel Foundation

Devin: *What is your superpower?*

Pia: *I think—usually, I have something to say.*

Now, as for me, connectivity is my superpower—making connections. It comes naturally to me. I find great satisfaction

137

in connecting people to one another or connecting people to opportunities, so I think that's a powerful and cool superpower.[12]

You can watch the full interview with Pia here: pia.s4g.biz.

Suzanne DiBianca, Salesforce, Chief Impact Officer

Devin: *Suzanne, as you think about your life, what is your superpower?*

Suzanne: *I don't think I have a superpower, really.*

I think maybe, if anything, my superpower is to sort of connect people to each other and then get out of the way. You know I have a fairly good intuition, and I've been able to build an incredible network. The executives and managers that I've been able to sort of put on boards of organizations that I've met and just get out of the way on that, I think they have built beautiful relationships, things I would never have thought of. So maybe if I have any superpower at all, it's just connecting like minds.

You can watch the full interview with Suzanne here: suzanne.s4g.biz.

Pia Wilson-Body and Suzanne DiBianca are near counterparts at Intel and Salesforce, respectively. Focused on using resources created by large companies to do good, both are leading innovative efforts to make the world a better place—each using their "connecting" superpower to do it.

"I believe a zip code does not determine brilliance, but the zip code can determine access," Pia says, referring to access to quality education and

---

[12] Because the focus of the book is on personal superpowers, a portion of Pia's response was not included above, but for completeness, the deleted portion is provided here: "Ok, I will answer that two ways, Devin. I will answer Intel's superpower, and Intel's superpower is passion. Employees are passionate about what they do, and they're just as passionate about volunteering in the community. I could not leave this interview without saying that. It is in their DNA. As I shared earlier, our employees volunteered a million hours around the world, and so the superpower for Intel is passion."

other resources. She is proud of Intel's efforts to invest in STEM (science, technology, engineering and math) education for underserved communities. Over two years, she says, Intel donated over $1 billion to such programs.

"Impact takes collaboration," she says. The power of collective impact comes from working together. You can see how it makes sense for the Intel Foundation to play a funding role with operational nonprofit partners across the country to support disadvantaged people. It would be more complex and likely less productive for Intel to spool up operations to do the same thing the nonprofits are already doing. Collaboration works.

Suzanne leads similar programs at Salesforce. Today, she's focused primarily on investing a portion of the Salesforce Ventures fund in social impact. Among the investments she guided is one in Classy, run by Scot Chisholm, featured in Chapter 46.

Another company she guided funds to is Measurabl, led by Matt Ellis. His company makes software for large companies to measure their energy usage. Salesforce uses it and now reports its energy use in its annual 10K filed with the Securities and Exchange Commission and available to the public.

Suzanne says she is particularly interested in finding more companies fighting climate change that can qualify for funding. She sees urgency in the fight.

At Salesforce, Suzanne led an effort to encourage startups to donate to nonprofits. Called Pledge 1%, the goal is to get companies to donate 1 percent of equity, time, product and profit to nonprofits. Note that donating the equity takes advance planning from the early stages of the company. Thousands of companies have now taken the pledge, potentially committing billions of dollars to charity.

Now, leading the company's impact investing program, she sees a blurry line between for-profit and nonprofit opportunities for social good. Companies like Classy and Measurabl epitomize for-profit companies that have significant social impact.

Suzanne committed to making investments with her fund allocation on a non-concessionary basis, with no financial discount for social impact. The fund's return targets are high. She's proud to report that, at least in the early going, results from the impact investments have matched the returns of the rest of the fund.

Both Suzanne and Pia have seen how their ability to connect people and organizations has served them well and has made a difference in the world. You can do the same.

How to Develop Connecting as a Superpower

Connecting is a superpower. Pia highlights her native ability, saying, "It comes naturally to me." Similarly, Suzanne mentions her "intuition" as helping her make good connections with impact. If you've felt that way before, perhaps you can make it your superpower, too.

On the other hand, if a cocktail party or reception sounds like torture to you, the guidance in this chapter may help you to overcome a limiting factor in your impact. Read on!

People like Pia and Suzanne know that everyone has needs, and everyone can meet someone else's need. Think about that. The wealthiest, most successful and powerful people face difficulties, and the most challenged among us have resources to solve someone's problem.

If you start with the above premise, you recognize that connecting people isn't selfish or a burden but can be a real benefit to both, unlocking your ability to make connections.

There are lots of ways to make connections. Let's consider three levels of introduction: an email, a conference call and a meal.

Level one is email. Most of the time, making an introduction won't require more than an email connecting them. There are two scenarios to consider.

First, you may realize or learn that two friends or colleagues of yours don't know each other and should. In that case, you should write an email introducing them, providing each with a short paragraph about the other, perhaps linking to bios or LinkedIn pages.

Second, you may get a request from someone, possibly an acquaintance, for an introduction to someone you know. Here, the best protocol is a bit different. Rather than send an email introducing them to each other, you may wish to ask the requestor, Bob hypothetically, to provide you with a forwardable email of no more than 300 words. Here is a specific outline for what you should ask that Bob include in that message.

1. *Express thanks.* Yes, I'm suggesting you should ask Bob to thank you at the top of the message. The primary reason is to provide a context for reminding you to whom he hopes to be introduced, as in, "Thanks for offering to connect me with Susan."
2. *Explain purpose.* Encourage Bob to explain in simplest terms why he is interested in connecting. There is no wrong reason, so long as it is true. If the purpose is "I want to pitch my services as a juggler for birthday parties," you may decide not to forward the message (unless you know Susan is looking for one).
3. *Introduce yourself.* Bob must provide a one-paragraph introduction, perhaps linked to a more extended online bio or LinkedIn page.

When you receive the email, you have three options.

1. If the email reveals a purpose or background you don't want to endorse, you have the option not to proceed.
2. If the email and purpose are good, but you don't want to pressure Susan to respond to Bob, forward it without copying Bob and let him know you've done so.
3. If the connection now has your strongest endorsement, forward the email with a copy to Bob to signal to Susan that you trust and endorse him.

Level-two connections involve getting on a call, perhaps a video call now that the pandemic has trained us all to use Zoom. To schedule it, send an email similar to the first type described above in level one. To make this easy, consider including three possible times more than 72 hours in the future for such a call. Be thoughtful about time zones and whatever else you may know about your friends' schedules.

Level-three connections involve getting together in person, most likely over a meal or at least coffee. Consider whether you should start the process by speaking by phone with each of the participants to gauge their interest and explain why you think the meeting will be helpful to them. Once you've laid that groundwork, you can schedule using a similar email approach to a level-two connection.

When you convene your level-three meeting, you can lead it using an approach that follows one of the level-one email models above. You may want to introduce them to each other and allow for an organic discussion. On the other hand, you may know that one has a clear purpose for the other, perhaps asking for a significant donation to an organization you support. In that case, it would make sense for you to use the email forwarding model, where you give the hypothetical Bob the floor to make his pitch to Susan.

Following these simple guides, you can flex your connecting muscle to become more like Pia and Suzanne. With practice, you can build your intuition until it feels like connecting is something you're born to do. When that happens, you've got a new superpower.

Marc Alain Boucicault

Chapter 38: Connecting the Dots - Marc Alain Boucicault

Devin: *Marc, what's your superpower?*

Marc: *I don't think I have any. I really think anyone can do what I'm doing. If you are passionate, if you are disciplined, if you know how to connect dots, I think you can do anything that I'm doing right now.*

Building this company, honestly, was a bit unique, and I did not think I was capable of doing it until I actually started putting the dots together. The guy [Roy Glasberg] at Google that I met amazed me when he said the following, "I don't have any superpower. I just know how to connect the dots." And that resonated with me. And when I came back to Haiti, I tried to reach out to sponsors, people who were sponsoring my social venture, to find that interest in a person that really would like to be able to help you. Not asking too much, but just a little bit. And you, your job is to connect those little bits all together because there's no big money in Haiti that you can just tap your hand into and build the company and build the 800 square meter space just like the one we have today.

It takes time, patience and being able to connect the dots. If I would say I have a power, maybe that's what it is.

You can watch the full interview with Marc here: marc.s4g.biz.

Marc Alain Boucicault is a Fulbright Scholar who worked for the International Development Bank and the World Bank as an economist at the outset of his career. As much influence and power as that gave him, he felt he could make a bigger difference as a social entrepreneur, helping build the tech industry from the ground up in his home country, Haiti.

From scratch, he built Banj, a co-working facility and business accelerator with high-speed internet access for tech entrepreneurs in Port-Au-Prince. He held a variety of events and brought entrepreneurs into the space to begin building tech companies.

Then, without warning in one evening, a riot in this capitol city focused on removing the president included a rampage of destruction that destroyed every physical manifestation of the community he'd built over the previous two years. His business was gone.

At that point, he thought there would be no way to recover. Building it once had represented a herculean task. He couldn't see a way to recreate it all.

For once, I suspect, he was happy to be wrong. The community he had built, including an international network of support, including sponsors and investors, rallied around and helped rebuild the facility.

Today, he boasts that more than 7,000 people have attended events there. Hundreds of entrepreneurs have received support, coaching or a place to work. Among these are 40 tech companies getting mentored and cultivated to build a tech economy in a country without one.

When I first spoke to Marc before the riot, he described his superpower as connecting the dots and explained the process by which he'd connected with people and obtained from each some token of value. In that conversation, however, he didn't fully appreciate how important that network of connected dots was.

When the riot left Banj in ruins, the network returned. One by one, the sponsors and donors, the entrepreneurs and everyone else in the community returned. They helped organize a crowdfunding campaign to restore the building, and before long, it happened.

"That's when I realized this is stronger than me," Marc says. Once assembled as parts of the organization, the connected dots represented something more than he had appreciated, certainly something more significant than and somewhat independent of himself.

How to Develop Connecting the Dots as a Superpower

Marc and I reconnected so I could learn how you can learn to connect the dots the way he does. You can see the powerful interview here: marc2.s4g.biz.

Marc provided four specific steps for growing your ability to connect the dots.

1. *Be genuine.* "Be yourself." His advice may seem almost counterintuitive. Many people counsel doing what seems almost the opposite, to fake it in some way. Marc says that being genuine is a way to connect with people that moves them quickly to trust you, making possible the little investments and commitments that may make all the difference. Just "living your dream" inspires people in ways that they may not fully understand. They just believe that they are dealing with the real you, not a fake or a phony.
2. *See potential.* Marc likes to see everyone as having the potential to help. Sometimes, that potential is immediate, sometimes further into the future. He recommends thinking about your needs on a granular scale. Rather than feel you need $1 million to move forward, think about all the individual things you will do with that money: office space, computers, desks, paint, carpet, accounting help, legal help, mentoring, etc. With every person you meet, think about how their lives, interests and abilities align with your needs. Identify the potential intersection.
3. *Give back.* As you develop relationships with people, look for ways to reciprocate kindness. You want to build a connection that doesn't feel like a one-off transaction but instead creates a role for them in your story. Create a role for yourself in their story. By finding ways to show appreciation, you write a shared plot that intertwines your parts. Marc's participation in this book exemplifies his effort to build on the relationship we established when I wrote about him for the first time more than three years ago for Forbes.
4. *Use social media.* Having followed him for years, I think Marc truly is adept at this. Using platforms like Linkedin and Facebook, you can connect with people you might never have a chance to meet in any other way. He belongs to several groups, each of which has a presence on social media. He uses these groups to network, meeting people who take an interest in him and find small ways to be helpful. Don't underestimate the power of social media.

As you think about these steps, you'll see how you can apply these in your work. Finding the help you need in smaller chunks, sometimes in kind rather than in cash, may be a vital adjustment for reaching your goals. Whether or not you can achieve Marc's proficiency at connecting the dots to make it a superpower, even incremental improvement could make a difference.

Valerie Red-Horse Mohl

Chapter 39: Teamwork - Valerie Red-Horse Mohl

Devin: *Valerie, what is your superpower?*

Valerie: *You know, I love that question because I come from a background that almost feels counterintuitive to the SVC (Social Venture Circle) culture in the sense that it's not something that's talked about a lot at SVC, and that is my sports background. I, myself, am not an amazing athlete at all, but my husband played NFL football, and consequently, all three of our children, fortunately, inherited his genetics. And they all played sports at a fairly high level. And I think you know that my daughter at Stanford now plays beach volleyball. If you talk to me for any more than five minutes, you will know that because everyone in my office is a little sick of hearing about beach volleyball.*

But what I've learned over the years as the quintessential team mom and I've also been a little bit of a coach here and there and just a cheerleader, a huge fan. And I'm talking about painting myself in the colors and having earrings and clothing and all of that. I've learned that there are some really important lessons from athletics that we need to apply in our lives, in the world and in business. And that really is around teamwork and collaboration and kind of working together with our strengths. And I often use my husband when he's in an audience with me for my example. He is a former offensive lineman for the Oakland Raiders. He is six foot six and 300 pounds, although he says he's now 280. So, I'll give him that. He's about 280. But regardless, for those of us that don't weigh anywhere near that, it's big. And then I say, you know, you, as a coach or a team personnel director, you would never put my husband as a running back. You know he is an offensive lineman. That's his strength. That's what he's built for.

I think my superpower in the role that I sit in is to be able to pull together our team, to be able to empower them, what their strengths are, and also not just within SVC, but looking at the ecosystem. We have so many wonderful partners out there that we're all kind of doing the same work. We have the same goals and the same passions. And I have started initiatives where we're working together towards common goals. And I think that's what we need to do. So, I'm a collaborator, and I'm a team mom.

You can watch the full interview with Valerie here: val.s4g.biz.

Valerie Red-Horse Mohl is a social entrepreneur, filmmaker and nonprofit leader. Today, she serves as the East Bay Community Foundation CFO, managing $700 million for social impact.

As a filmmaker, she directed the acclaimed film *Mankiller* about Native American activist Wilma Mankiller, the first woman elected as the principal chief of the Cherokee Nation. As a child, her family was forcibly relocated from Cherokee land in Oklahoma to the San Francisco Bay area. She participated in the Native American occupation of Alcatraz, an effort to enforce tribal rights under existing treaties. Following her political career, she returned to activism. President Clinton awarded her America's highest civilian honor, the Presidential Medal of Freedom. Valerie's film brought her inspiring story to a new, larger audience.

Valerie started her finance career while studying filmmaking at UCLA. After working for a large investment bank, she launched her own and completed $3 billion in financings, primarily for businesses owned or led by

Native Americans. "It was by far the hardest thing I've ever done in the workplace, to raise the capital, start an investment bank on Wall Street and try to survive and thrive in a very male-dominated and a sexist, racist environment, in all honesty," she said.

More recently, as the executive director for Social Venture Circle, a national association of social entrepreneurs and impact investors, she helped increase diversity, equity and inclusion. In effect, she moved the organization to better align its actions with its values by elevating the participation of Native Americans.

Despite having an impressive career, when asked about her greatest accomplishment, Valerie did not hesitate to boast about her role as a mother. Raising three children is not just a point of pride. They motivate her work, inspiring her to make the world a better place for them.

It is mainly through her experiences guiding the three through sports that she developed her teamwork superpower. You can learn from her experience to make it your superpower, too.

How to Develop Teamwork as a Superpower

Valerie has made teamwork a hallmark of her career, putting people in roles where they are a good fit, empowering people to be successful and collaborating to accomplish organizational and societal goals. She got her first inside look at sports when she married Curt Mohl, who played professional football.

You can do the same—even if you aren't married to a retired pro football player.

Here are some steps you can use to build a team and develop Valerie's leadership skill for yourself.

1. *Lead.* Teams need leaders, so be one. The 1950s model of one man directing operations through command and control is dead. Leadership requires you to walk your talk and build personal relationships with your teammates. Establishing trust is paramount.
2. *Communicate.* To create the dynamic you want on a team, you'll need to establish both formal and informal channels of communication with a goal toward transparency. Communication will include team meetings, email or a platform like Slack or Basecamp, Zoom and the telephone. If you have a team workspace, be sure to look for ways to foster informal communication in its design.
3. *Build.* Teams don't just happen. To convert a group into a team, you'll need to actively choose to do team-building exercises, hold

retreats, strategy sessions and have fun building trusting relationships.

4. *Organize.* As Valerie points out, you've got to put people in positions where they can use their greatest strengths. Empower them to use their superpowers! Sometimes this can require you to shuffle the deck. If someone isn't a fit for the team, look for an opportunity to help them leave to a new position and preserve their dignity.

5. *Unify.* Ask the team to define ground rules, including how the team reaches decisions, builds consensus and what to do about making decisions when there is no consensus. Establish with the team's permission when you have the authority to make a decision or overrule the group consensus. Once established, respect the rules faithfully.

6. *Target.* With the team, set goals for the team to accomplish collectively. Identify the roles and objectives for each member.

7. *Measure.* Having set goals, measure performance. Hold the team and its members accountable. Celebrate success. Embrace failure as an inherent part of a worthwhile goal.

8. *Appreciate.* Thank every team member for their contributions. It is impossible to express too much gratitude. No one wants to be taken for granted or be unappreciated.

With these simple steps, you can convert your group, department or division into a real team that can accomplish big things. As a leader like Valerie, you can make teamwork a superpower.

Part 4 - Leadership

While virtually every superpower in the book improves leadership ability, some discussed in this section can be viewed as being primarily useful for leaders. For instance, empathy and problem-solving skills can be used in many ways, but learning to motivate and inspire others is essential for leaders.

Samson Williams

Chapter 40: Developing Leaders - Samson Williams

Devin: *Samson, what is your superpower?*

Samson: *Oh, my superpower is helping smart and amazing people be even more smart and amazing. I only know that and have that prepared because I'm writing a book, A Survival Guide for Furloughed Careers. Right now, 800,000 federal employees are furloughed, which affects another 2 to 3 million people just in the D.C. area. So, it occurred to me that my superpower was helping smart and amazing people be more smart and amazing. I don't necessarily want to be out front, but if you give me some pom poms, I will start cheering. Every quarterback needs someone to block and tackle. So at the end of the day, I prefer to block a tackle, but if necessary, I will lead.*

You can watch the full interview with Samson here: samson.s4g.biz.

Samson Williams is an anthropologist. While true, that last sentence is so incomplete as to be almost irrelevant. As the Crowdfunding Professional Association president, he is a nationally recognized leader on raising money for startups, including via blockchain technology. He is also an adjunct professor at Columbia University and the University of New Hampshire Law School, teaching cryptocurrencies.

Raising capital is critical to the success of entrepreneurs, including social entrepreneurs, women and BIPOC entrepreneurs as well. As a leading voice in the arena, he is helping these change agents succeed.

He is also the author of several books, including *Race in Space*, which warns leaders to avoid and eliminate historic racist precedents in the booming space economy. The book is evidence of his forward-thinking activism.

Samson's influence is not limited to the U.S. He's advised business and government leaders in several countries, especially in the Middle East. Much of his career has focused on crisis management and disaster preparation. His goal has been to help organizations survive crises.

Throughout his career, Samson has been working to help people succeed, "helping smart and amazing people be even more smart and amazing." Now he considers it his superpower, posting that near the top of his Linkedin profile. You can do it, too.

How to Master Developing Leaders as a Superpower

It was only after doing it for decades that Samson recognized his superpower. You can choose to develop the same power.

His success at helping others lead has driven him to become a leader himself. Still, his focus remains on supporting other people.

He notes two areas he uses to help people reach their potential.

1. *Cheerleading:* Sometimes, an intelligent, impressive individual lacks only recognition. By acknowledging their accomplishments publicly and encouraging them privately, you can help them lead. One key to being a successful leader is having followers. The first one is the hardest to find. You can be the first follower, giving a leader credibility and momentum.
2. *Blocking and Tackling:* There is nothing worth doing that doesn't involve work. Sometimes the leaders you'll want to develop will need you to do some of that. By stepping up to complete tasks that move the ball forward, you can help leaders drive progress.

Looking at Samson as a role model, you can see how sharing what he knows, teaching and training people is a key to his superpower. He is an author, consultant and adjunct professor. In all those roles, he's helping leaders learn what he already knows.

You may not be a professor, author or consultant, but you can still share what you know with others. Samson is active on social media, especially LinkedIn, where thousands of people follow his professional insights. You can start there. Share your wisdom on social media.

Samson is strategic about his writing. His books comprise many of his social media posts. He sometimes writes drafts of chapters for his books as Linkedin posts. This way, he shares the information in two completely different settings, the first allowing him to receive feedback. Your social media posts can be the first draft of your book, too.

You can develop leaders. Like Samson, you can help "smart and amazing" people become more so. You can make this your superpower, too.

Dennis Whittle

Chapter 41: Empowerment - Dennis Whittle

Devin: *Dennis, what is your superpower?*

Dennis: *I don't know if I have any superpowers, but to the extent I do, I think it's getting people to believe that they can achieve things that they never thought were possible. If you come into our office here, we have people that are—I hesitate to say this on a podcast but could easily be leaders at the fanciest Silicon Valley companies—and they didn't start out that way. But now, they are superheroes of design, superheroes of tech, superheroes at due diligence, superheroes at financial management, and machine learning. I like to think that with a couple of exceptions that we enabled them to be that. So I'm not sure I have—I maybe have a superpower of helping other people find their superpowers. I'm extremely proud of the quality of what we do, made possible because people can reach for things and achieve things that they never believed were possible.*

You can watch the full interview with Dennis here: dennis.s4g.biz.

Dennis Whittle has spent his career driving impact, becoming an impressive serial social entrepreneur. Starting in the Philippines, working for USAID, he transitioned to the World Bank, where he spent 14 years rising to senior ranks. Dennis then partnered with Mari Kuraishi (see Chapter 27) to launch Global Giving. He subsequently started Feedback Labs and, most recently, Normal>Next.

Dennis and Mari, who married while they both worked at the World Bank, catalyzed over $500 million of impact to nonprofits working in lower-income countries worldwide. It began after they created a development marketplace as a competition among nonprofits to garner funding from the World Bank.

At the end of that competition, a woman who had competed for the funds complained about not being funded. They encouraged her to come back in a few years when the World Bank might repeat the competition. She was not pleased. When she pointed out that the World Bank was not the only game in town, Dennis said it hit "like a shot between the eyes." Within six months, they launched Global Giving.

Dennis led the new nonprofit for a decade before turning the reins to Mari, who likewise led the crowdfunding platform for almost a decade.

As a way to return the favor of scholarships he'd received to attend both the University of North Carolina-Chapel Hill and Princeton, he spent a few years teaching at those schools and others.

Then, he launched the nonprofit Feedback Labs, encouraging other nonprofits and government agencies to implement meaningful feedback programs to improve their results as measured by those they serve.

His current social enterprise, Normal>Next, is a team of "seasoned executives, entrepreneurs, and young leaders from diverse backgrounds dedicated to helping the world thrive through profound economic, social, and environmental turbulence."

He never stops innovating ways to make the world a better place. Along the way, he's mastered the leadership tool of empowering his teammates to develop their own superpowers. You can master this ability, too.

How to Develop Empowerment as a Superpower

While CEO and subsequently as a board member at Global Giving, Dennis helped team members develop a wide range of professional skills, including finance, information technology, machine learning and design. He developed empowerment as his leadership skill.

Similarly, you can learn to empower others as your superpower. Here are some tips to help.

1. *Determine the goals.* Before you can effectively empower someone, you need to understand where they're going. Find out what their goals are both operationally and for their careers. In

some cases, it will be your role to help establish the functional goals; when that is so, be as collaborative as possible to get shared targets.

2. *Identify the strengths.* When working to empower a colleague, particularly to help them develop their superpowers, jointly identify their strengths. A 360 feedback process, where colleagues, friends, subordinates and supervisors provide insight about strengths, could be a starting point.

3. *Delegate authority.* When you have control over a colleague, be sure to delegate authority to match their responsibility. Nothing limits progress and growth more than to have assigned duties without being allowed to make the required spending and related decisions.

4. *Be supportive.* Without attempting to micromanage your colleague's work, be supportive. Provide positive encouragement when the going gets tough. Respond reassuringly to trips, falls and stumbles. Help them up. Be sure you both see failures as learning experiences.

5. *Give compliments.* You can increase empowerment by helping your team believe in themselves and recognize their capabilities and progress. When you see it, call it out honestly and emphatically.

6. *Show gratitude.* You can't thank people too much or too often. Some studies suggest that people hear the fewest expressions of appreciation at work. That is where it is likely most deserved. Giving thanks will make you both feel better.

7. *Celebrate success.* When your team members accomplish objectives, react appropriately. Match every success to the volume it deserves. You shouldn't ignore small victories, but they don't require the same level of celebration that big wins get.

8. *Be patient.* Real empowerment takes time. Be patient with yourself and with your team. Dennis talks about the sort of progress he observed over two decades in leadership at Global Giving. When you look back over similar periods, you could see matching progress.

The tips above can help you be more like Dennis, developing the ability to empower your people to master their own superpowers. What a great superpower!

Barry Rassin courtesy of Rotary International

Leesa McGregor

Chapter 42: Inspiring People - Barry Rassin and Leesa McGregor

Barry Rassin, Rotary International, 2018-19 President

Devin: *President Barry, what is your superpower?*

Barry: *Our theme in Rotary this year is to "Be the Inspiration," and I'm very fortunate that when I speak with the Rotarians, I'm able to give a message that really seems to get them in their hearts. And we're seeing them do more than we've seen* *before. So, inspiring people and getting our Rotary Clubs motivated not only to continue doing amazing work–they know that our priority is to eradicate polio. And they keep asking what's next. Yeah, just let's finish polio. Let's not have a "next" yet.*

You can watch the full interview with Barry (and Bill Gates, see Chapter 60) here: barry.s4g.biz.

Leesa McGregor, Author

Devin: *What's your superpower?*

Leesa: *I think my superpower is inspiring change, I realized, through speaking, and I've been doing a lot of speaking even recently; it's just my passion. I really love to share with people how they can be part of the solution. You know, I always talk about how right now the world's biggest problems are actually the world's biggest opportunities, their future solutions. Right? And so, if we can align ourselves with being part of the solution, we've got an opportunity to create change in all these areas. And sometimes we have to reach crisis point, whether it's, you know, all of these things we're very aware of–climate and democracy and all of these things–that that's an opportunity. The breakdown leads to the breakthrough. And I truly feel that we're on this edge of incredible evolution if we can step into the narrative of where we're going in the future. That's what I get most excited about. So, I'd say my passion and my purpose–and my superpower is inspiring this positive change and helping people to understand how they can be part of this movement.*

You can watch the full interview with Leesa here: leesa.s4g.biz.

Barry Rassin, Past Rotary International President, based in The Bahamas, and Leesa McGregor, a children's book author and social entrepreneur based in Canada, share a passion for and a proven ability to inspire others.

Barry, who served as the President of Rotary for the 2018-19 year, had previously led as President and CEO, the Doctors Hospital Health System in the Bahamas. He remains on the board to this day.

As Rotary's President, he was not only responsible for inspiring 1.2 million Rotarians in 35,000 clubs around the world, he was charged with raising $50 million to match a fundraising challenge grant from the Gates Foundation that would triple Rotary's $50 million by adding $100 million. He was successful at both.

Just weeks after his tenure ended, his country was devastated by Hurricane Dorian, the strongest hurricane ever to strike land in the Atlantic Ocean. It packed sustained winds of 160 miles per hour and gusts well over 200 miles per hour. About 45% of homes on Grand Bahama and the Abaco were damaged or destroyed.

Barry leveraged his skills, network and influence to bring relief. He helped organize a flotilla of 25 boats to evacuate hundreds of Abaco residents who lost their homes to the storm. Rotary set up an emergency water treatment plant, and Rotary Clubs adopted shelters to support the families through the crisis. Barry became an international voice for the country's efforts to attract needed emergency funding.

His entire life of service in Rotary and his professional experience as a hospital administrator prepared him for a moment where he could make a life-saving difference.

Leesa McGregor is a social entrepreneur. She was teaching her child to read with traditional alphabet books, using words like "A is for Apple," when she began thinking about creating a more impactful alphabet book. She wrote a children's book called *A New Alphabet for Humanity*.

As she wrote the book, she worked to incorporate messages inspired by the United Nations Sustainable Development Goals. Passionate about the environment, she also used the book to teach kids about caring for the planet.

Leesa, who partnered with me on a course teaching the basics of social entrepreneurship (still available on Udemy), has built a publishing business around the book. Not only has she sold 60,000 copies of the book, but the company offers a whole suite of related products, from coloring books to kits for teachers.

She is indeed proving to be inspirational.

Barry and Leesa are inspirational role models. Following their example, you can make inspiring others your superpower.

How to Develop Inspiring People as a Superpower

Barry inspired people to donate millions to polio eradication and then used his superpower again to help people in The Bahamas recover from Hurricane Dorian. Leesa has used her superpower to inspire children and their teachers and parents more meaningful lessons than just the ABCs.

Here are some tips to help you inspire people.

1. *Walk the talk.* Here's the hard reality: If you are not walking your talk, living your message and doing what you're asking your followers, supporters or employees to do, they'll see right through you. You can only inspire others to do what you have done or are doing. Barry can raise money to fight polio because he's given so much. Leesa can teach kindness to others and the planet because she lives that every day.

2. *Empathize.* To inspire someone, you've got to know them. Before you give a speech, write an email or create a video, get to know and appreciate your target audience. Before launching a new campaign with your existing team or fans, talk to them about it. Learn and understand how they feel so you can implicitly or explicitly address their concerns as you move forward.

3. *Set aspirational goals.* You've got to define what winning means in your situation. When Barry raises money for polio, he describes the ultimate goal as the eradication of the disease. His definition of winning may also include raising money to meet the Gates Foundation match this year. Raising $50 million in a year is a big but achievable goal. It marks progress toward a more aspirational goal of eradicating a disease for only the second time in history. You can use the same model in your work with a big goal that may take a long time and a more achievable goal for a set time frame.

4. *Be enthused.* You've got to share your excitement and optimism. Leesa is a natural at this. She is so enthusiastic you can't say no to her. She exudes passion for her purpose and draws you into her world. You can do the same.

5. *Exercise patience.* Real change takes time. Rebuking people for failure or slow progress will not inspire better behavior. Give yourself and others time to act. In the interim, repeat steps one through four above. Eventually, your efforts will likely inspire the results you seek.

As you can see, you can be as inspirational to others as Barry or Leesa. By following the steps above, you can inspire people to change the world. The good they do because of you will be like the ripples spreading across a pond after you skip a stone across it. Inspiring others can be your superpower.

Part 5: Passion

Passion can be described in a variety of ways, but you'll likely agree that success at big things requires it. The next three chapters explore ways changemakers are using and developing their passion.

Rebecca Masisak by Kit Karzen

Chapter 43: Caring - Rebecca Masisak

Devin: *Rebecca, what is your superpower?*

Rebecca: *Hmmm, well, I don't know for sure what I would call my superpower because everything that is a true thing about your personality, sometimes it's good, sometimes it's not, right? I think one thing I'll say that's kind of defining about me is that I was told once and at the age of 22 in my first performance evaluation that I cared beyond all reasonable amounts of caring. And I think that pretty much does describe me. That has made me sometimes work too hard on a problem that I was never going to solve. And at the same time, it has really helped me not let anything too daunting keep me from going forward. So I think that's something that anyone who knows me will kind of find permeated in my work. Couple that with a lot of energy, and you kind of, hopefully, get somewhere.*

You can watch the full interview with Rebecca here: rebecca.s4g.biz.

Rebecca Masisak is the CEO of TechSoup Global, a nonprofit that helps other nonprofits around the world with technology and related support. She has led the organization as its co-CEO or CEO for 15 years. Today, she is leading one of the most innovative nonprofit initiatives in history.

TechSoup is the first nonprofit to use Regulation A+ to conduct a securities offering open to ordinary investors, not just wealthy people and institutions. The nonprofit divided the offering into three parts, with different terms based on the size of your investment. Those who can invest $50,000 or more get 5 percent interest. Those who can invest $2,500 get 3.5 percent. Finally, those who can invest just $50 earn 2 percent. All the loans are paid back over five years.

TechSoup supports over a million nonprofits around the world, often with free or low-cost resources. Rebecca believes that every $100 invested in the offering will help the nonprofit distribute an additional $47,000 of technology-related resources worldwide.

Impact investing, the concept of putting money to work to do good while earning a financial return, is much younger than TechSoup. It is a remarkable sign of leadership for Rebecca to move forward with this direct public offering creating impact investment opportunities for everyone. She is hoping to raise a total of $11.5 million, which would increase the organization's impact by several billion dollars per year.

Rebecca is thriving in her role in no small part because she cares "beyond all reasonable amounts of caring." She takes responsibility for the organization and is undaunted by challenges. You can copy her caring and make it your superpower, too.

How to Develop Caring as a Superpower

For Rebecca, caring is not just about her mission to support civil society globally but more about taking responsibility for the organization. She admits she sometimes takes on problems she can't solve, but it more often means difficulties do not dissuade her.

In truth, I could have grouped this superpower in the part of the book about altruism because she cares about her mission and the people she serves. I could have lumped it in with persistence because she is undaunted. I've chosen to include it with passion because the word she chose to describe her superpower, "caring," is about the feeling that motivates her, which is closely related to passion.

Sometimes, I've seen this attribute described as parenting. As you think about how a mother or father cares for their child, you see some hints that can help you emulate Rebecca. Nurturing parents often demonstrate the following behaviors with absolute commitment based on their love for their children.

1. *Provide.* Parents provide food, clothes and shelter for their children. You can apply that to your projects by working to ensure they get

the resources they need. Rebecca is working diligently to complete the $11.5 million direct public offering to help TechSoup grow.

2. *Defend.* You've likely heard the phrase "mama bear" used by mothers to describe their tempers flaring when defending their children. Fathers do it, too, but when they get angry protecting a child, dads are just called dads. Social impact projects, nonprofits and social enterprises all need defending. They tend to be vulnerable like children.

3. *Support.* Much of a parent's role is just being there to provide support. As you work to grow your impact project, you've got to be there. To emulate Rebecca, you have to show up, even when it isn't convenient.

4. *Guide.* Parents educate and inspire their children, teaching them principles to guide them to and through adulthood. You can probably think of essential lessons you learned from your parents. Part of caring for your project will be guiding the people on your team.

Still, your projects aren't your children. Some projects just don't work, and even you will admit that you should scrap them. You'll know when you're caring enough when you find terminating a project is emotionally painful—but not impossible.

Extending the metaphor, note that Rebecca manifested this trait early in her career. Her boss assigned her the projects she cared so much about at age 22. She adopted them and cared for them with the same passion as she did the projects she led and created on her own later.

If this chapter resonates with you, see if you can make caring your superpower. If not, using the four nurturing tactics listed above can at least help you grow more successful impact projects.

Premal Shah

Chapter 44: Passion - Premal Shah

Devin: *Well, Premal, what is your superpower?*

Premal: *I don't know what my superpower is, but I will say that something that I know, I feel like [what] I bring to the group at Kiva is when I get excited about something, you know, it's almost like for me it's like, oh wow. I think it's just passion. It's just like I know I get carried away by my own passion and a belief in possibilities and a curiosity about how you might get what's seen as difficult done—breaking things down into smaller problems and just working away at it and letting the work teach us. I think there's something around passion and possibilities. I don't know if it's a superpower, but it's something that I think I get to bring every day to the team at Kiva.*

You can watch the full interview with Premal here: premal.s4g.biz.

Premal Shah is the co-founder and for 13 years served as the president of Kiva, the crowdfunding site for microloans for underserved people around the globe. During his tenure as president, Kiva made over $1 billion in loans—96 percent of which was repaid by borrowers that many considered unbankable.

Premal's overarching goal at Kiva was to change lives, not just make loans. He didn't measure his success by the scale of the enterprise but the impact loans made on lives. To ensure that borrowers benefit from loans, Kiva works with field partners who use the Kiva platform to raise the money.

Kiva screens field partners on two primary criteria, the first being financial sustainability. Kiva loans come with zero interest and no fees, but Kiva hopes to return the funds to the lenders. Field partners typically charge a fair interest rate but may need to raise additional funding to cover operating costs. Kiva wants to be sure the field partners have the financial ability to run the programs supporting borrowers.

The second criterion is the social impact of the field partner. Impact is a function of three factors, including 1) who the partner serves (are they genuinely underserved?), 2) how the partner measures impact and 3) the impact measured. By scrutinizing the impact data, Kiva can choose partners who do the most good.

Typically, field partners are doing an excellent job of measuring that borrowers increase their income by more than the cost of servicing the debt, so net income increases, often permanently.

You can become a Kiva lender with as little as $25. As with any crowdfunding site, you can choose a person to back. If you lend a multiple of $25, you can diversify your portfolio by lending $25 each to multiple borrowers. You will receive no interest, but 96 percent of the time, you can expect to get your money back, allowing you to revolve your loans to serve people continually.

Scaling up that model is how Kiva has helped millions of people with billions of dollars of loans.

When Premal stepped back from his operational role at Kiva in 2019, he described how he discovered the common goals, dreams and hopes that all humans share. That clarity motivated the creation of Kiva.[13]

Premal describes his passion and excitement as his superpower. By bringing enthusiasm and energy to the team day in and day out for over a decade, he led the creation of an organization that helped millions of people—and will continue to do so long into the future. You can do it, too!

How to Develop Passion as a Superpower

You may be tempted to think that you either have passion or you don't and that you can't develop passion as a superpower. That's not crazy, but

---

[13] Premal Shah, Kiva Blog, "Thank you – a letter from Premal Shah, Kiva Co-founder & President," https://www.kiva.org/blog/thank-you-a-letter-from-premal-shah-kiva-co-founder-president.

there are some things you can do to find and share your passion to be more like Premal.

Start by finding things that fire your passion. In Chapter 34, in the context of finding your purpose, you read about finding your passion. If you completed the exercise described in that chapter, grab your notes. If not, consider just doing this simplified version now.

This exercise could be challenging. If it would be safer for you to skip to avoid painful triggers, or if you need someone to talk this through with you, be sure to take care of yourself. If and when you're ready, write down the things that make you angry or sad. Think about the times you got so mad you yelled at someone, broke something or hurt your hand, smacking it against the wall—or worse. Next, think about what triggered real tears—a painful sadness that made you feel desperate to either be alone or find a loved one for a hug. Then, write down the triggers that upset you. These likely connect you to your passions.

If you are already working for a cause, look for ways to connect your passions to your work. For example, you may get upset when you feel disrespected. Is there a way to see how the people you serve might feel the same way? Could you be the chief respecter in your organization? Whatever your passions, see if you can channel them for good in your work.

Next, you need to think about how you share your passion positively. Premal uses his passion, expressed as excitement, to amplify his "belief in possibilities and... curiosity." Sometimes your passion will surface as sadness. It is okay for people to know you care deeply about the problems you are trying to solve. Don't be ashamed of those feelings. Your passion may rise at times as anger. Be careful when that happens. It is difficult to harness anger for good, even when your emotions are justified. Let the anger fuel your effort but be cautious about expressing anger as colleagues may feel inappropriately targeted even if you don't direct fury at them.

There are times when your passion comes as bursts of optimism and energy. Share *that* abundantly to help your team feel your passion and confidence for making a difference in the world.

By finding and sharing your passion, with Premal as a role model, you can make it your superpower, too.

Darrin Williams courtesy of Southern Bancorp

Chapter 45: Passion for Helping People - Darrin Williams

Devin: *Darrin, what is your superpower?*

Darrin: *No, I don't profess to have any superpower. We just have a passion for helping people who are doing good. And again, I'm inspired by the 380 plus people that work here at Southern day in and day out. They care about the communities that they serve. They care about the customers they serve, and, you know Devin, most of the employees grew up in rural Arkansas or rural Mississippi, small-town America. They care about these flyover states, states that many don't think about, and they want those communities to thrive. They don't want to live in the big city. They want to make a home in small-town America, and they want those communities to thrive. And so I'm committed and inspired by them to work and to make sure that that happens.*

You can watch the full interview with Darrin here: darrin.s4g.biz.

Darrin Williams is the CEO at Southern Bancorp, one of a short list of banks in America focused on serving the genuine needs of low-income customers. Fighting to end predatory banking practices like payday lending, Darrin's bank strives to help people.

169

In 2019, I spent a day with Darrin. What a day! We began with a tour of Clarksdale, Mississippi, to visit some of the people and projects financed by Southern Bancorp and ended the day with some of the bank's executive team over dinner in Little Rock, Arkansas. I got a first-hand look at the impact of positive banking.

Clarksdale is in the Mississippi Delta, one of the most economically challenged regions of the country. About 80 percent of the population is African American. Lush and green when I visited, it is also prone to flooding. Clarksdale is also among the places that lay claim to being the home of the blues. Before the pandemic, you could find a live performance somewhere in town every night of the year.

During my day with Darrin, the most shocking visual was of the local Paramount Theater financed by the bank. (The playwright Tennessee Williams saw his first movie there.) Together, the banker, the borrower and I visited the theater, stood on the stage, and looked into the pile of rubble that had been a roof months earlier. The roof had collapsed onto the seats. Darrin remained proud of the loan even as the collapse pained him as it did the borrower, Bubba O'Keefe. Bubba hoped to rebuild, recreating the largest theatrical venue in town.

Paramount Theater

With other local partners and financing from Southern Bancorp, Bubba converted an old building in town into a boutique hotel, where I stayed for about $100 when I visited. Clarksdale is on a long-term upswing, at least in part, because Darrin brought his bank to make a difference.

Later, we met with Jennifer Williams (no relation to Darrin), a teacher in Clarksdale with three college degrees who fell prey to payday lending. Southern Bancorp offered a free course in escaping payday lending, which included refinancing some outstanding payday loan balances. Darrin introduced us proudly, even though Jennifer is no longer a Southern Bancorp customer. She's just much better off because she was at a critical moment in her life.

Darrin is applying his passion for helping people to his work in demonstrable ways. While he says it's not a superpower, I'd say helping Jennifer escape payday lending and financing a building with no roof contradicts that argument. You can channel your passion for helping people to create a superpower, too.

How to Develop Passion for Helping People as a Superpower

Darrin is an impressive guy who had a remarkable legal career before joining the bank, including running the Arkansas Attorney General's office and serving in the state legislature. Still, you can emulate him and build your passion for helping people as your superpower.

His superpower requires holding two opposite-sounding but harmonious ideas in your head at the same time. First, you need to remember that you sometimes need help. Second, you need to be confident that you can help other people.

By remembering that you sometimes need help, you can better empathize with the people you want to help. If you see them not as inferior beings in need of help but as peers whose pain and suffering are like yours when you are in trouble, you will fire up your passion for helping them.

Then, by being confident of your ability to help people, you avoid feeling frustrated and helpless, even in the face of daunting challenges. The best way to develop this confidence is to practice. So, go help people.

The more you help people, the more your confidence will grow. So, too, perhaps will the tendency to forget the first principle—that everyone, including you, needs help at times. Keep that reminder written down. Whenever you want or need help, think about how you're just like the people you serve.

That approach is what I've observed in Darrin. He is confident of his ability, using the bank, to help people. That is his focus. That said, as successful and educated as he is, Darrin sees everyone as his equal.

By following Darrin's example, you can make a passion for helping people your superpower.

Part 6: Honesty

Does the need for honesty go without saying? Perhaps it could, but some of the changemakers featured in the book noted that some form or part of it was their superpower. In the next two chapters, you'll read about how you can make it yours.

Scot Chisholm

Chapter 46: Transparency - Scot Chisholm

Devin: *Scot, what is your superpower?*

Scot: *Good question. I would probably say I'm a really transparent guy, to a fault sometimes, but that can be—could be—considered a superpower. I'll give you an example from the early days. When we were starting the company out, we would produce this report for people that had invested in the company and whatnot. And we sent it to all the employees, including the interns. It had all our information and financial data, cash in the bank—everything. You'd think that we would have stopped that at some point, but we didn't. We keep sending the same reports every—now we're about 240 people here. And they get the same level of information in a lot of ways that our investors do, that I do. And that level of transparency, even though I've been criticized sometimes for it, has built an amazing amount of trust internally with the organization. So, folks know kind of the state of the business, and they feel like they've got a seat at the table. That's one positive way. But, I think that being transparent and communicating honestly and openly about where we're at and what we're doing has been—I would say—I've never really thought of it as a superpower but maybe some secret sauce in helping to grow the company.*

You can watch the full interview with Scot here: scot.s4g.biz.

Scot Chisholm is the founder and CEO of Classy, a social enterprise and certified B Corp that helps nonprofits in various ways, primarily to raise money, now totaling over $2.5 billion.

Classy uses several labels for its fundraising approaches, including crowdfunding, giving days, peer-to-peer fundraising, online fundraising, etc. The bottom line, however, is clear. Classy works for nonprofits.

He decided to launch Classy after seeing how broken fundraising could be. He organized a pub crawl to raise money to fight breast cancer in honor of his mother—a two-time survivor. But, shockingly, the nonprofit he chose refused to accept the money! He knew then there had to be a better way.

Evidence that he did create a better way continues to mount. We visited less than three years ago to celebrate Classy having raised $1 billion for its nonprofits. Now past $2.5 billion, the growth is continuing. One aspect that helps is $300 million per year of recurring gifts.

Before reading more, please step back. Take a deep breath and think about what Scot and his team have done. From a standing start a decade ago, the company helped nonprofits raise billions of dollars. Think about all the good that has happened, the hungry people who have been fed, the unsheltered who have been housed and the sick who have been healed because of Classy. The impact is immeasurable.

Scot's transparency is a superpower. You can make it one of yours.

How to Develop Transparency as a Superpower

Scot built his superpower from the beginning at Classy by disclosing the state of affairs to employees. That's a big deal. Having been around many startups, I'm confident that the financial reports weren't all rosy. But, by sharing the difficulties as well as successes, he built credibility with employees, shareholders and customers that helped him build the company.

Scot defined transparency as "communicating honestly and openly." You can do that, too. It will take courage (see Chapters 48 and 49).

Here are some steps you can take to develop transparency as a superpower in your operation.

1. *Walk the talk.* If you're going to make honest and open communication a theme, you have to behave that way. You've got to demonstrate congruence between what you say and what you do.

2. *Report results.* Like Scot demonstrated at Classy, you need to report your results as broadly as you have your organization's goals. People will want to know how well they've done compared to the objectives they've worked to achieve.
3. *Share the org chart.* When you're the boss, you've got to be sure everyone understands the organizational chart. This isn't about who's the boss. Instead, it is about who does what. People will have a hard time collaborating if they don't even know who is responsible for which function.
4. *Open your door.* Transparency requires you to observe an open-door policy. When your team members need to ask you a question, you've got to be available. I've never seen this better implemented than at Cornell's Johnson Graduate School of Management. The professors were expected not to have office hours because they were effectively required to be available to the students every minute they were in their offices. Almost unbelievably, the professors observed this practice. Students loved it.
5. *Explain decisions.* It is easy to assume that your team will correctly infer your logic for making decisions. However, if you do, you'll often be wrong. When you make a decision, explain it. You can also indicate whether the decision is cast in stone or open for review after a probationary implementation.
6. *Accept feedback.* Get ready. When you open your door and explain your decisions, you'll get some feedback. Not all of it will be positive. But, the better you accept feedback when you hear it, the more transparent you will seem (and indeed be).
7. *Respond to requests.* You won't always be able to do what your colleagues ask of you. Still, if your teammates know the organization's financial situation and how you make decisions, you'll be wise to respond consistently and appropriately to the requests you receive.

Using these tips, you can develop transparency as a superpower in your organization, just as Scot did at Classy. Then, wherever you fit in the org chart, you can apply these principles to those within your purview (be careful to respect the confidences your leaders have entrusted to you). If your behavior is different from the rest of your organization, you'll likely see your practices praised and ultimately adopted more widely.

Daryl Hatton

Chapter 47: Trustworthiness - Daryl Hatton

Devin: *Well, Daryl, what is your superpower?*

Daryl: *I seem to have the ability for people to trust me quickly. I've earned that because, based on results, I'm quite trustworthy. To gain someone's trust, I give them mine. When I do this, I'm able to make an authentic connection with people really quickly. It helps me bring out the best of who they are, and I like doing that. And it's a ton of fun to be able to have that kind of connection with people.*

You can watch the full interview with Daryl here: daryl.s4g.biz.

Daryl Hatton is the CEO and founder of FundRazr, a leading crowdfunding platform for nonprofits. FundRazr is a division of his company ConnectionPoint. By innovating in this space, he has helped individuals and nonprofits improve and even save the lives of both animals and humans.

Daryl admits he launched the business in 2008 primarily because he saw a business opportunity. That changed for him and his team when they received a Christmas card from a couple who had used the platform to raise about $3,500 for airplane tickets, thanking them for helping save their daughter's life.

It turned out that the family was in Hawaii, living "off the grid" and without health insurance when their daughter was diagnosed with leukemia. As a veteran, the father got a military hospital in San Diego to agree to treat her. Lacking funds, they used FundRazr to quickly raise money to travel. After being seen and with treatment started, the doctor told the parents, "it was a good thing you got here when you did; she might only have lived another day or two."

That Christmas card changed Daryl's perspective. It changed the team as well. From that point forward, they recognized the social impact and made that their primary motivation. Daryl says he now plows all the profits back into the business to continuously improve it.

Daryl's innovations include tools to make it easy for nonprofits to raise $500 at a time. He points out, as an example, that many nonprofits seeking to rescue animals from being killed have budgets around $1 million annually and help 2,000 pets, meaning each pet saved costs about $500.

Raising $500 is relatively easy compared with raising $1 million, in part because a $50 donor is much more motivated to help with the small raise rather than the big one. That $50 donor feels like they make a big difference toward a $500 goal but an insignificant one toward a goal of $1 million. But conducting thousands of fundraisers each year can be daunting. By creating tools to make that efficient, FundRazr is helping nonprofits address their funding needs in a novel way.

Daryl says his superpower is trustworthiness. As one who is helping nonprofits raise money, that makes perfect sense. If you listen to what he's saying, however, you begin to appreciate that he's really talking about building personal relationships more than profitable ones. While building profits is essential, one of the lessons many have taken from the COVID-19 pandemic is the value of relationships. You can learn to make trustworthiness a superpower to improve your personal and professional lives.

How to Develop Trustworthiness as a Superpower

Trustworthiness is a watchword for anyone working with money, so for Daryl, it is critical. Interestingly, he highlights how it impacts personal relationships. You can develop trustworthiness, too.

Being trustworthy includes authenticity. "Being yourself and authentic is one of the best ways to succeed," Daryl says. "It drives people crazy because it feels so risky at times." You may be able to relate to that. Most people feel social pressure to be and appear a certain way.

Here are six things you can do to develop trust.

1. *Trust others.* "To gain someone's trust, I give them mine," Daryl says. It is a team sport. While you become a bit vulnerable when you trust others, you encourage and empower them. By trusting, you implicitly invite others to trust you.

2. *Be honest.* Building a trusting relationship requires impeccable honesty. That doesn't mean you need to be brutally honest. You can give bad news tactfully. Say you're a vegetarian and a colleague gives you a donut with bacon, you can thank them for the kind gesture even as you note you won't be able to eat it. If you don't, another bacon-topped donut or a ham sandwich could appear in the future.

3. *Keep confidences.* In countless situations, information must be kept private. Sometimes it goes without saying. A member of your team takes time off for health reasons; that is their business to share, not yours—even if they share it with you.

4. *Be transparent.* It may seem out of place to highlight transparency immediately after reminding you to keep confidences, but openness builds trust. The key is to remember to share appropriately. Some things, like your blood pressure and your sex life, are private. But you can still safely share a lot of personal and professional information to strengthen trusting relationships.

5. *Be reliable.* There may be no better way to strengthen trust than to do or be where you promise when you promise. Whether it is arriving on time to a meeting or completing a project on schedule, being reliable will build your brand as a trustworthy person.

6. *Be humble.* At first, you may be wondering, "what does humility have to do with trustworthiness?" Sometimes, an honest assessment of the facts will conflict with your agenda. When you are willing to humbly acknowledge you're mistaken or have failed, you earn the trust of those who observe your actions.

By cultivating your trustworthiness like Daryl, you can make it a superpower that will help you change the world for good.

Part 7: Courage

Changing the world starts with changing yourself. Change requires courage. In the next two chapters, you'll read about impressive changemakers who have made courage a superpower.

Ina Pinkney courtesy of Rotary International

Chapter 48: Fearlessness - Ina Pinkney

Devin: Ina, what is your superpower?

Ina: Oh, I might have that Wonder Woman costume right under my top–I'm not sure. My superpower is that I'm fearless. I am never reckless, but I am fearless.

You can watch the full interview with Ina here: ina.s4g.biz.

Ina Pinkney began learning to be fearless as a childhood survivor of polio. Ina could climb the three flights of stairs to her assigned room but needed extra time, so school administrators allowed her to enter the building early. During fire drills, she was allowed to remain in the classroom. My mind can't help but wonder now if there had been an actual fire, would she have been allowed to remain in the classroom?

She remembers being bullied by other kids as a six-year-old. "I understood at that point that I could not cower but had to find some power to go up against that." She recognized that they were not kind, but she knew she would not treat other kids that way. She sees facing those bullies as the beginning of building fearlessness.

Ina had 21 jobs in her career. "I was fired from 19," she says. The pinnacle of her career was owning and running "Ina's," an American food restaurant in the West Loop Market District of Chicago, for 23 years.

Her fearlessness was critical to starting that business. She'd never run a restaurant before. Her only relevant experience was eating. "I knew that I could do it," she says. "I just knew it because I had seen everything around me, and I knew I could be better than that." So, she did.

After joining Rotary, primarily because of its global leadership in the fight to end polio, Ina found a new opportunity to use her superpower: public speaking. As a polio survivor, Rotary District Governors invited her to speak at District Conferences facing audiences of hundreds of people. The Governors expected her to motivate Rotarians to continue donating to a cause that was starting to feel endless.

Ina says it takes "fearlessness to stand up there and say, this is who I am. This is not who you think I am. This is who I really am." Rotary has rewarded her courage with more speaking invitations, including a prominent role in the 2018 World Polio Day, jointly hosted by Rotary and the World Health Organization.

Her work is bearing results. As of July 30, 2021, there have been just two polio cases from wild poliovirus globally this year.

Ina has taken control of her life, overcame her disability, and made a difference in the world of polio eradication because she is fearless.

How to Develop Fearlessness as a Superpower

Many people sometimes allow fear to prevent them from doing things they could do and want to do. Perhaps you have. If you would like to overcome a fear limiting your impact, success or happiness, Ina has a few insights for you. She joined me for a second interview you can see at ina2.s4g.biz.

Learn by Example

You don't need to go through everything Ina has to overcome your fear. Ina's solution is simple. Learn from the examples of the courageous people you know, from public icons to your friends and neighbors. Watch those who are doing what you'd like to do and repeat their steps.

"It takes less energy to be courageous than it does to be afraid," Ina says. Her favorite example of this is Oprah Winfrey, who was famously nervous about having her ears pierced. At age 51, after decades of worry, because she was afraid it would hurt, she got it done.

Think about the energy she wasted being nervous about two quick sticks that barely hurt and enabled her to wear earrings that are less likely to fall off—something that matters if you've got diamonds in both ears. Imagine how much less energy she would have used to have done it 20 or 30 years earlier.

Whenever you do something that requires more courage than having your ears pierced, chant the mantra, "I am more courageous than Oprah! I am fearless!"

Preparation

Ina used her superpower to go skydiving. While most people are reluctant to hurl themselves from a perfectly good aircraft, she says she felt only excitement and not fear as she did so.

Honestly, I was skeptical when she said so. I thought, of course, she was afraid. But she overcame it and did it anyway. Ina says she wasn't scared because she prepared.

She reminded me that she is "never reckless." She had talked to her friend, Julian, who helped with the jump. She knew everything to expect. There were no surprises. She even had a watch with an altimeter. She was ready. And she was fearless.

Ina uses that same approach to prepare for everything. When she enters a room, she stops at the doorway, assesses the room and prepares mentally for whatever may come. "I then own the room," she says. "I own the room because I have prepared myself for anything that could happen. People won't talk to me; people will ignore me, whatever. I walk into that room ready."

By following the examples of others and preparing for anything, you can overcome fear. Imagine what you could do if you weren't afraid. Now, do it!

Kimmy Paluch

Chapter 49: Recklessness - Kimmy Paluch

Devin: *Kimmy, what is your superpower?*

Kimmy: *I think my superpower is, I guess, we were being a little bit reckless, like I said. I think that with all entrepreneurship, sometimes you need to take leaps of faith. And I'm often one to be compulsive and take a leap of faith. And I encourage others to take leaps of faith on themselves.*

You can watch the full interview with Kimmy here: kimmy.s4g.biz.

Kimmy Paluch is the managing director of the pre-seed stage venture fund Beta Boom. She and her business partner and husband, Sergio Paluch, focus on investing in people in underserved communities and social entrepreneurs.

Having accomplished so much, Kimmy could be resting on her laurels. Instead, she is working to change the world. When I asked her about the most important lesson she had learned over her impressive career, she said, "find the thing that motivates you most and go for that."

For many people, that motivation would be selfish. Not for Kimmy. She notes that your legacy is what you leave as a result of your success. "I'm proud of all of my achievements, but I hold a much higher bar for what comes next."

"Do I use it for my own gratification or my own self-interests, or do I pay it forward?" she asks.

"When your goals are much bigger than yourself, you will have a lot more to be proud of."

Thus, focusing her work on helping overlooked entrepreneurs, some of whom look like her, has become her passion. She also sees it as an opportunity. If women and minorities are ignored by most venture funds—and the data overwhelmingly suggests they are—then investing in them could bring significant financial returns.

Kimmy doesn't just work to invest in underrepresented entrepreneurs but also to provide better support after funding. The work of entrepreneurial success doesn't end with a funding round; it begins.

An early Beta Boom investment was in Fiveable, a platform for providing Advanced Placement education to high school students. The founder, Amanda DoAmaral, is a young former Teach for America teacher who started offering AP help to students. She discovered there was massive demand for her help. With funding and guidance from Kimmy and Beta Boom, she converted her volunteer effort into a thriving social enterprise that has now reached 4 million students, made an acquisition and added Serena Williams's venture fund as an investor.

Kimmy describes her superpower as a "little bit" of recklessness. She says entrepreneurs need to take a leap of faith to succeed, and she's done that successfully. You can, too.

How to Develop Recklessness as a Superpower

In the last chapter, Ina Pinkney made a point to say she was fearless but not reckless. Kimmy owns her recklessness as her superpower. If you're an entrepreneur or aspiring to be one, you'll recognize that success requires taking risks. If that's reckless, then that's the deal. Get ready to leap!

For Kimmy, being reckless is about taking a leap of faith, betting on yourself and your team to accomplish something significant. Here are six tips to help you have the courage to take the risks required for success.

1. *Start where you are.* Where else would you start? The truth is, many aspiring changemakers and entrepreneurs wait to start and thus never do. They wish to be better capitalized, educated or experienced. But the moment never seems right, and they never execute on the dream. So, regardless of where you are, start.
2. *Calculate the risks.* When doing the calculation, remember GoDaddy founder Bob Parson's mantra, "They can't eat ya." Whatever the worst-case scenario may be, you will survive. Remember, too, that failure has another name: experience. Still, it is a good idea not to proceed blindly.

3. *Share ups and downs.* As you move forward, find ways to share both the upside and the downside risks. Your team, your financial backers, and even your customers can share in the benefits of your success and the downside if things don't work out. Sharing the risk can make an otherwise unwise risk tolerable or even appealing.
4. *Build on your strengths.* As you've been reading this book, you've identified several personal strengths. Some of these you'll build on to become even stronger. You may have identified a few weaknesses that you can remove or reduce enough to prevent them from limiting your success. Be your best self.
5. *Believe in yourself.* As you assess and polish your superpowers, take confidence. There are things you're good at doing. No one is a virtuoso at everything. You can take your strengths and do something that matters. Have faith.
6. *Leap!* There is a point in every business launch where there is a transition from planning to executing. Don't get bogged down in planning. Move as quickly as sanely possible to taking action. That leap could change the world!

When you learn to be a little bit reckless like Kimmy, you can leave a legacy bigger than yourself. You can own your recklessness and make it your superpower.

Part 8: Persistence

Persistence has a unique omnipotence. Persistent water carved the Grand Canyon. In the next five chapters, you'll read about people who used their persistence to change the world—and how you can learn to do the same.

Apolo Ohno

Chapter 50: Hard Work - Apolo Ohno

Devin: *Apolo, what is your superpower?*

Apolo: *I would say my superpower still relies on a foundational component of hard work. While that's a broad term, I think that we can talk about resilience and passion and hunger and grit and all those things that I think that we typically associate with maybe the Olympics or athletes and things that you have to do that are really challenging and hard. But what I have found, Devin, is that throughout my career, both during the Olympic space and also when I decided to retire and reinvent that the one foundational piece that I could always rely upon was hard work. And that was something that I don't think that I inherently had as a young child. My father had kind of instilled some of these principles associated with that broad term hard work when I was a child. But it wasn't until I really started to feel and see the type of long-term, consistent marginal increases in performance day over day that I would then have to compound over long durations of time where I would find that to be my superpower.*

And the reason why I say that is because I was not genetically gifted more than perhaps the top 10 or 15 or even 20 of the world's greatest speed skaters and winter athletes. So, I had to find other areas and mechanisms on which I could lean. There were many times where I looked at the competition and thought, they're better than me, they're faster than I am. They're stronger than I am. They're better genetically designed for this sport, inherently, just naturally more talented. So how do I compete with that? And I had to find areas where I found that maybe they weren't willing to go through. And so, you know, the saying goes, it may take me longer than the average bear, but I think the strength in that is, well, I can't always control the outcome. I am willing to throw myself headfirst into something. Maybe if it's not my greatest strength or my first natural inclination to be performing well at a particular task or sport or career, I think being able to face that fear and go through what they call the gauntlet is a superpower.

And I think we have seen this time and time again of those that we would optically view as being successful. And I think it comes down to that fundamental principle, right. You can plan--you can create these amazing kinds of vision boards, but there's no replacement for the day-to-day grind and consistency. And while others may do things faster or more effectively than you, over the long term and duration, if you stay consistent in those principles, I believe that that's where your real edge is going to come from. That's what I've found with me, is I believe in hyper immersion. I believe in super hard work. And while we cannot always control the outcomes, it's about how we perceive these challenges or so-called failures and then recalibrate them to figure out this is a challenge. This was a learning experience for me. I'm going to take this and grow from it. I'm going to take this and expand from this particular experience in my life. So everyone contains this ability inside of them. That's the beautiful part; hard work is there for anyone to really understand and realize. And with the access to information that we have today, there are no more boundaries. There are no limitations. It's up to you as the sole driver of your life ship to figure out which direction you'd like to steer this thing.

You can watch the full interview with Apolo here: apolo.s4g.biz.

Apolo Ohno is America's most decorated Winter Olympic Athlete of all time. He competed three times in the Winter Olympics (2002, 2006 and 2010) as a short-track speedskater winning eight medals.

Many people believe they work hard. It's cliche. But Apolo is the expert. No one is more qualified to model and teach you hard work.

Today, he leverages his skills and experience in many ways, including as a television commentator for the Olympics. He is a New York Times bestselling author, a business leader and philanthropist. He deploys his superpower to improve his performance in all these areas.

Apolo deployed hard work at a fresh, new level for his third Olympic Games. The sport of speedskating was evolving, with the top athletes physically different from his first Games. They were becoming "skeletal" above the waist with all their muscle in their lower bodies. Many were drawn to the sport because they had been born with this body type. Apolo had to rebuild his body. He lost weight and gained strength, keeping him at the pinnacle of competition. He won three medals at those 2010 Games, becoming the most decorated Winter Olympian in U.S. history.

Today, Apolo deploys all his energy to accomplish a single objective. "My main fundamental goal at the end of the day is to help others succeed." Helping you learn to model hard work is one way he does that.

Building your capacity for hard work will help you make this a superpower, one that will enhance all your other strengths as well.

How to Develop Hard Work as a Superpower

Apolo had to learn hard work in much the same way you have. He trained for his first Olympic Games in 2002 as a teenager, providing him an opportunity to learn a skill that would serve him for the rest of his life, not just in speedskating.

Apolo shared some specific, actionable ideas to help you learn how to make hard work a superpower.

1. *Prioritize process over prize.* Apolo learned early on that at some point, you have to shoot the arrow. Once released, it will go where it will. You no longer have control over it. On the other hand, the

process of preparation helps you become something better. By focusing on the process of becoming rather than on the prize, you will get the full benefit even if the arrow doesn't hit the bullseye.

2. *Deploy your introspection.* Effort made in the wrong direction is wasted. As you do the hard work of changing the world for good, remember to ponder what you're doing and why. Periodically, take the time to ensure that your actions align with your fundamental values and guiding principles. Make sure your passion and purpose guide your effort. Apolo would remind you that you can't work hard all the time and get a benefit. Periods of rest and planning are required for the hard work to yield the desired results.

3. *Embrace the challenge.* Doing things that matter, especially those few people do—like competing in the Olympics or curing cancer—is difficult. There will be challenges, problems and setbacks. Coping with those issues will make you stronger and more capable. Embrace the challenges as a central part of your effort.

As a bonus, Apolo notes that incorporating play into your work makes it more enjoyable and sustainable. Put another way, having fun will help you do more reps. The more you do, the better you'll become.

When other people brag about their hard work, compare their experience to Apolo's. He may be uniquely qualified to teach you how to do it. Implement his three lessons into your life, and you can make hard work your superpower. Think, too, about how much stronger your other superpowers will be if you amplify them with hard work.

Dr. Bhavya Rehani

Chapter 51: Not Quitting - Bhavya Rehani, MD

Devin: *Bhavya, what is your superpower?*

Bhavya: *My superpower? I think that I don't give up. I keep dreaming, and I keep doing my best to find solutions for different kinds of problems that arise every day because of the kinds of operations we have in different countries. So, I think that has helped me because the challenges are so big. But just having that faith that, you know, we have to find a solution to make this work has helped us incredibly.*

You can watch the full interview with Bhavya here: bhavya.s4g.biz.

Bhavya Rehani, MD, is the CEO and co-founder, with her husband Dr. Ankur Bharija, of Health4TheWorld, a nonprofit focused on education for healthcare workers worldwide, especially in rural villages.

Bhavya is a Harvard-trained neuroradiologist currently practicing at the University of California San Francisco. Ankur is on the faculty at nearby Stanford. Talk about a power couple. It is inspiring to see people of such ability and opportunity devote themselves so fully to nonprofit work.

Their goal with Health4TheWorld is to provide quality training to healthcare providers free of charge. Using live streaming technology, they gather top doctors in their fields, many from the U.S., to offer live virtual global training to professionals participating remotely. As the internet begins reaching the four corners of the earth, it is exciting to imagine remote health clinic workers watching live training from Stanford, UC San Francisco, Harvard or Johns Hopkins.

The database of recordings is impressive. Bhavya and I spoke when stroke training was the focus, even then anticipating the addition of a wide range of topics. Today, the platform offers recordings on 100 subjects, including COVID-19, oncology, cardiology and pulmonology.

Some of the videos are for community health workers, enabling them to help their patients manage illnesses like diabetes, diarrhea and birthing complications. Lives will be saved directly as a result of the Health4TheWorld training.

Additionally, Bhavya has led the translation of many of the videos into Spanish, making them accessible to Hispanic healthcare providers. The organization will add more languages in the future.

Bhavya recognizes the scope of the problem and the scale required of Health4TheWorld to match it. She emphasizes teamwork in accomplishing the task, highlighting the contributions of the doctors who provide the free training.

Throughout her years of training, Bhavya repeatedly had to demonstrate an ability not to quit. She is applying that superpower to growing Health4TheWorld. You can learn from her to make not quitting your superpower, too.

How to Develop Not Quitting as a Superpower

As you read and reflect on Bhavya's explanation of her superpower, you see hints of several superpowers in this book coming into play. She talks about dreaming about solving problems, hinting at her optimism and her ability to solve problems. The phrase "we have to find a solution" ties into the persistence and tenacity we cover in this section of the book.

Just below the surface of her singular superpower of not quitting, there are several that give her the strength not to quit. Nonetheless, you can still see that not quitting is a uniquely powerful ability.

There's another essential reality to consider. People quit all the time. Quitting is often good. It is wise to quit smoking. It is best to walk out of a stupid movie. It is even appropriate to stop working on a social impact effort that is failing or has served its purpose. The vital issue is knowing when not to quit.

Here are some questions you should consider asking before you quit your social impact effort when facing a challenge.

1. *How big is this challenge compared to your project?* Imagine you learn that you need a permit that will take three weeks to obtain and

costs $1,500. For a car wash fundraiser to raise $500 this weekend, it could spell doom. On the other hand, the permit would have somewhat different implications for a health clinic with a $20 million capital budget and a $5 million annual operating budget. When a challenge comes up, put it into context and perspective.

2. *Does the data match your mood?* Bad news can be emotionally discouraging. Sometimes, the emotion you feel may not align with the data. For instance, if a donor were not only to reject your funding request but also insult the project, you would likely feel pretty disappointed. Check the data. Have other funders supported the project? Have other people praised it? It's normal to feel upset by unkind feedback or a significant setback, but don't give up if the data points you toward success.

3. *Who can help?* When something discouraging happens, you may feel isolated or alone. Give some thought to who can help. Start with someone who can give you good advice and an encouraging word.

4. *What information do you lack?* When a problem arises, it may seem overwhelming. Be sure to identify the missing information. Your imagination or experience could cause you to exaggerate the challenge or even misunderstand it. Learn what you don't know already about the problem, and a solution could become evident.

5. *Is there a natural law that prevents a solution?* When Elon Musk virtually reinvented space travel at SpaceX, he became famous for asking his team to explain the laws of physics that prevented them from doing what he asked. When you face a problem, check to see if some natural law will prevent you from succeeding. The answer will often be encouraging. Practical solutions must exist or at least be possible.

Asking these questions can help you frame a problem so that quitting would seem either absurd or intelligent. Act accordingly. Most often, if you're tackling a worthwhile social issue, you'll find the answers will guide you to keep going.

You can emulate Bhavya. You can make not quitting your superpower.

Monique Ntumgia

Chapter 52: Overcoming Adversity - Monique Ntumngia

Devin: *Monique, what is your superpower?*

Monique: *My ability to just get through the worst challenges. Trust me; I can get through just about anything. Trust me. I personally don't know how I do it, but I've been through thick and thin. But there's—I don't know how my brain works— but there's always a solution to everything. That's my superpower. If that's a superpower, I just could get through the worst of scenarios. That's me.*

You can watch the full interview with Monique here: monique.s4g.biz.

Monique Ntumngia was orphaned as an adolescent and has grown into a tech-savvy social entrepreneur, working to empower women and girls in her home country of Cameroon even as she fights climate change and poverty. She founded Green Girls Organisation as her vehicle for change.

Using Green Girls, Monique provides rural and semi-rural communities with solar electricity, just enough for lighting, and biogas from agricultural and human waste for cooking. She helps the women and girls in the community learn to assemble solar lamps from kits she provides. They then share revenue on a 70/30 basis, where the local women keep the majority of the revenue. The women also sell the biogas on the same revenue share program.

Now just 31 years old, Monique's work is reaching scale. The organization has trained over 4,500 women and girls and has created solar electric or biogas systems or both in 48 African communities. Yet, ironically, some of the residents she helps with solar live below power lines they cannot access.

Along the way, the organization has created 3,500 jobs she describes as "eco-sustainable." Her efforts have improved literacy by 65 percent. Health outcomes have improved 70 percent. Sexual harassment has dropped 75 percent. Finally, deforestation in her communities is now at an all-time low. Understandably, she has received numerous international awards and recognitions.

Overcoming adversity is the appropriate superpower for one who endured so much at such a young age. Monique experienced "tribalism" and conflict among various ethnic communities. At age 12, when her father died, her mother "lost everything" because she was not of the same ethnicity. Not much later, her mother died of breast cancer.

The odds were against her. That she survived is remarkable. To have become such an influential leader is extraordinary. Monique's superpower is worth emulating.

How to Develop Overcoming Adversity as a Superpower

Can you think of a challenge you've faced and overcome? I'm confident you can. At the same time, you may live your life—as almost everyone does—constrained by fear of present or pretended challenges. Learning to overcome adversity better can be powerful for you.

In a follow-up conversation you can watch here, monique2.s4g.biz, Monique provided some insights into how you can strengthen your power to overcome adversity. Here are the ideas I extracted.

1. *See the positive.* Monique's first rule is to see the positive and focus on that. Imagine how she felt as an adolescent who had lost her parents and whatever financial resources her family previously had. Circumstances forced her to face challenges most people don't overcome. One aspect was focusing on the positive.
2. *Find supporters.* As an extension of the above, Monique has identified people who support and help her. She nurtures her relationships with them. She's not talking about mere fans or followers. As a sign of her wisdom, she sees that helpful people offer her positive criticism.
3. *Ignore naysayers.* At the same time, she sees that some people cannot share her vision or mission. They want to see her stumble, fall or fail. She ignores them. You likely have some of these in your

life, too. Take her advice. Ignore them. Some could be family members or friends you can't cut out of your life, so you may need to find the courage to ignore their negativity even as you maintain a relationship.

4. *Know yourself.* Monique emphasized and re-emphasized the idea that you must know yourself. She describes it as the beginning of wisdom. Here's the real gem. She says, "You cannot change what you don't know." That profound insight can help you develop every superpower in this book.

5. *Accept yourself.* While she hastens to add that she has changed, she suggests we start by accepting ourselves and our limitations. You can't be two people. There are many facets to who you are—some you love, some you wish to change—but the reality is you are the composite of all those things. Still, accepting yourself does not mean you cannot change or should not change. You start where you are, not where you wish you were.

6. *Take care of yourself.* You can't pour from an empty vessel. You can't overcome adversity if you don't take care of yourself. Monique struggled so much during the pandemic she entered therapy and is grateful for it. She's learning these principles of self-care strengthen her ability to keep doing good.

7. *Find purpose.* Monique had developed a passion for changing the world to better provide for women and girls from an early age. She credits this passion or sense of purpose with helping her to overcome the challenges she faced then and the ones she faces now. You can find your purpose in the depths of the challenges you face. Seeing her mother treated unfairly when her father died helped her find her feminism. That kept her going. When you find your passion, it will help you overcome your challenges, too.

Everyone is different. Some of Monique's ability to overcome adversity may be circumstantial. Still, you can learn to overcome more significant challenges than you've faced. You can do things you may not believe. Even if you can't make Monique's superpower your defining characteristic, you can learn to do better by taking her advice. Increase your human potential by lifting the limits that constrain you.

Chris Soukup

Chapter 53: Super Vision and Relentlessness - Chris Soukup

Devin: *Chris, what is your superpower?*

Chris: *I think a couple of things I would offer as an answer to that.*

First, I feel like I have what I would call "super vision," and I pride myself on being able to see the things that other people may miss—the opportunities that aren't as obvious to the rest of the world. But I create a space there for our community to grow and to build.

The second thing is I would say that what I would call my relentlessness and just perseverance and just being very passionate about what we do and getting up every day with a renewed commitment to achieving the world that we know is possible, not just for the deaf community but for all people with disabilities.

You can watch the full interview with Chris here: chris.s4g.biz.

Chris Soukup is the CEO of the nonprofit Communication Service for the Deaf. The organization provides video sign language interpretation enabling deaf people to communicate with virtually anyone. He remembers when this wasn't possible, and his deaf grandparents would visit his home so his hearing mother could make phone calls on their behalf.

Being deaf continues to be unfairly treated in the United States and around the world. Chris was sensitized to this reality when his grandfather lost his farm because the banker couldn't believe a deaf person could operate a farm. Today, approximately 70 percent of deaf people are unemployed or underemployed.

Inequity motivates Chris. He uses the nonprofit to advocate for deaf and hard-of-hearing people. For instance, the organization worked with Uber to incorporate tools making it easier for deaf people to drive and for customers to interact effectively with them. When we spoke, he boasted that Uber had already hired 10,000 deaf drivers.

Chris is a third-generation deaf person. More than 40 years ago, his father, Ben, founded Communication Service for the Deaf, which Chris now leads. He hadn't anticipated taking over for his father as he grew up, but he joined the organization after graduate school and worked his way up to CEO.

The community Chris represents is more diverse than it once was. When he was born, he notes, the community could be divided into two related but distinct groups: the deaf and the hard of hearing. Today, because of technological advances, especially cochlear implants, new clusters are forming, including people who use the implants to hear and identify as deaf. Chris does his best to foster a sense of community among all the segments and advocates for their interests.

Chris is aided in his work by his superpowers, "super vision" and relentlessness. Never fear; you can develop these, too.

How to Develop Super Vision as a Superpower

First, let's look at how you can develop super vision, or the ability to see what others miss.

Drawing on the work of psychologists, Pulitzer Prize-winning journalist Joseph T. Hallinan wrote a brilliant piece on the difficulty of seeing what others miss.[14] His surprising conclusion was that the novice might have the advantage in seeing what the expert misses.

---

[14] April 18, 2014, Joseph T. Hallinan, Psychology Today, "Seeing What Others Miss," https://www.psychologytoday.com/us/blog/kidding-ourselves/201404/seeing-what-others-miss/

Experts, it turns out, are in some ways constrained by their more profound knowledge. Within their sphere, they know the patterns, the rules and the way things work. That competence begins to form a box that limits the options they consider.

On the other hand, a novice lacking the information that forms the box can see something that in hindsight may be evident to everyone but that experts missed.

In some ways, that resembles the role of the CEO. Although the leader of an organization may be a genuine expert in one or two areas of the operation, they may be novices in most relevant disciplines. Therefore, the key to seeing what others miss may be looking through the eyes of a child.

So, Chris may be able to see what others miss precisely because he's not an expert in every discipline. He may not be able to code. He may not be able to do graphic design. Legal work may fall outside his domain. And maybe that is what defines his capability to see what others miss. He sees with the eyes of a child.

In other words, the key is to look outside the box the experts are likely to construct to constrain or limit your thinking. Don't be duped. Look outside the box. There you'll find the superpower "super vision."

How to Develop Relentlessness as a Superpower

Chris notes that being relentless is another key to his success in making the world better for his community. You can develop that same ability.

Chris draws a clear connection between his relentlessness and his passion. His passion motivates his perseverance. That makes perfect sense; being relentless is about working at something despite challenges, even failures. The key is to find the motivation to continue despite the pitfalls. For Chris, that is passion. Learn more about developing passion in Part 5.

Here are some additional tips to help you master relentlessness.

1. *Don't fear failure.* You can't avoid small failures along the path to success. Embrace them as milestones along your way to having the impact you seek. Learn from each mistake.
2. *Keep learning.* Don't just learn from your mistakes. You can probably avoid some errors by learning from people who've done what you're doing, been where you're going or have at least tried. Read great books. Listen to powerful podcasts. Talk to experienced advisors.
3. *Look forward.* To be relentless, you must keep your attention on the future. If you spend too much time looking back, you'll be distracted. You cannot get back the weeks, months or years you

spent on a project. In finance, we call it a sunk cost if you cannot recover it. Ignore it and move forward.

4. *Simplify and focus.* Complexity will challenge you and make continuing your work more difficult. You have to keep your focus on a simple goal and strip away things that distract you. In some circumstances, you may need to jettison projects that otherwise may be worthwhile if the primary goal you relentlessly seek will suffer. You know the kiss principle: keep it simple, stupid.

5. *Try.* "You miss 100 percent of the shots you don't take," Wayne Gretzky said. Remember, you don't determine the outcome. You control the input. Put in the effort. Try. Then see number 1 in this list.

By following these steps, you can be relentless. You can make relentlessness your superpower.

LeAnn Thieman

Gary White

Chapter 54: Tenacity - LeAnn Thieman and Gary White

LeAnn Thieman, Author

Devin: *What is your superpower?*

LeAnn: *My superpower? That's a really good question. Maybe tenacity. My husband might call it stubbornness; I call it tenacity. We'll go with that.*

You can watch the full interview with LeAnn here: leann.s4g.biz.

Gary White, CEO of Water.org

Devin: *Gary, what is your superpower?*

Gary: *I think it probably does go back to that tenacity, right? I think that's something that's been in me for a long time. It's maybe a boring superpower, I guess. But to me, if I deeply believe that what I'm seeing or the insight is real and it can be extremely powerful, then I'm not going to give up, right? And to me, that tenacity of one—just the pure injustice of this, right? We should have solved water and sanitation more than 100 years ago. We still see millions of people dying from water-related disease and not having the dignity of a toilet. That, to me, is just unacceptable. And I think that's what I draw on in terms of tenacity. It's like there's no excuse. You know, when the solutions are at hand, and we know how to solve this, there's no excuse for not making it happen. And that's the source of the tenacity for me because we need to do this, and we can do it in our lifetime, and that is so solvable. Right? I mean, what we've done is create a system where the poor can now meet us halfway. We don't have to raise a trillion dollars —which is what it would take in charity to solve this crisis. We can use that philanthropy catalytically and leverage this capital from the bottom up. And if the poor are out there willing to meet us halfway, then it's even less excusable that we should not tackle this problem and get it done with the wealth that we've been able to concentrate in this world.*

You can watch the full interview with Gary here: gary.s4g.biz.

LeAnn Thieman and Gary White are two of the kindest, most soft-spoken people I've had on my show. They share the superpower of tenacity. Before you dive into learning how to be more tenacious, please take a few minutes to understand what they do with theirs.

LeAnn is a bestselling author and sought-after speaker who started her career as a nurse. Her world completely changed as a young woman when she purchased a dozen cupcakes at a fundraiser for Friends of Children of Vietnam.

The organization primarily worked to find homes in the U.S. for orphans who American soldiers fathered. Before long, LeAnn had not only joined the group but had organized a chapter in her home and was planning to adopt one of the children.

When the organization had six babies ready for adoption, she said, "I agreed to fly to Vietnam and escort them back to their adoptive home, the United States. But between the day I said I would go and the day before I arrived, the bombing went from 100 miles from Saigon to right outside the city limits."

Suddenly, everything had changed. President Ford approved "Operation Babylift." LeAnn would help bring home 300 babies. She was there for just five days. She and a few colleagues loaded babies three-to-a-box on a C 141 cargo jet and headed for the United States.

Among the babies was Mitch, who, though just a toddler, unmistakably volunteered to be her son. "He literally crawled across the room into my arms, my heart and our family," she says.

After 18 years, she wrote down her story and got it published. When she started getting invitations to speak, her response was, "About what?" People, mainly from the nursing community, wanted to hear about her lessons from Operation Babylift.

So, she prepared a speech and then wrote a book, *Balancing Life in Your War Zones*. She built her business around it.

Then, LeAnn submitted her story to Jack Canfield for inclusion in a *Chicken Soup for the Soul* book. Canfield accepted the submission. Then she started writing other people's stories for inclusion in the series.

Canfield later called her and asked her to co-author *Chicken Soup for the Nurse's Soul*. She did, and it reached number 17 on the New York Times bestseller list. She went on to write several other books in the *Chicken Soup* series.

She also wrote *SelfCare for HealthCare* as part of a training program for nurses that she provides over a year. The book, with its 12 chapters, focuses on a new self-care habit each month.

Now, she uses the book, along with other materials, to help nurses. She includes emails, videos and on-site progress charts in her program. The results, she says, are impressive, showing a 16% reduction in sick days and a 13% increase in retention. By helping healthcare workers care for themselves, she helps millions indirectly.

Interestingly, she shared that more than 20 years ago, when the kids were moving out of the house, her husband anticipated she would take up quilting. I'm so glad she didn't!

Gary White founded the nonprofit Water Partners to supply water worldwide to people who lacked access. More than a decade ago, he had the opportunity to collaborate with Matt Damon, who had launched the nonprofit H2O Africa with a parallel mission. Before long, they merged the organizations. Matt remains fully engaged, and Gary runs the organization.

Over the years, the organizations have helped millions of people gain access to clean water and toilets. Gary, and other experts, have seen that the number of people lacking access to clean water is shrinking and now represents less than 10% of the global population. However, about one-third of humans still lack proper sanitation.

In recent years, Gary and Matt have led an initiative to test a new model. In addition to their philanthropic efforts to provide water and sanitation, they've created an impact investing model paired with micro-lending programs. The fund lends money to organizations that provide tiny loans to people to buy and install a toilet or access a municipal water system.

Micro-lending for toilets is a novel approach to the problem. Micro-lending has been used for decades to help people in poverty borrow money to purchase income-generating assets like chickens, pigs and tiny retail kiosks. The model presumes that generating new income was a necessary outcome of the loan for the borrower to earn the funds to repay it.

Water.org's Water Equity program has demonstrated that low-income families can save money by legally tapping into a municipal water system to avoid paying higher costs to water vendors.

Women, who comprise most borrowers, also place high value on toilets, which allow them to avoid open defecation at night. Going out at night offers a sense of privacy because they can't easily be seen, but it put them at risk of sexual assault.

Because of this, women often borrow the funds from loan sharks and ultimately pay usurious interest. Gary and his team provide capital raised from investors to organizations that fund the purchases with fair interest rates, making repayment easier and safer. The funds are then returned to Water Equity and then the investors.

Gary gets excited about this program because it can scale rapidly. When a wealthy person donates funds, they limit their giving to maintain their wealth. The same person keeps virtually their entire wealth tied up in investments. Water Equity gathers investments rather than donations, allowing the organization to grow more rapidly. As it attracts more capital, Water Equity's loan program will let the nonprofit help more people.

The program requires low-income families to bear the cost over time. As Gary sees it, this isn't a downside. Given that they are willing to do so, Gary is happy to continue building the program to help more people.

Gary's tenacity is tied closely to his motivation to help people access water and sanitation. "We still see millions of people dying from water-related disease and not having the dignity of a toilet. That, to me, is just unacceptable. And I think that's what I draw on in terms of tenacity."

You can model the tenacity of LeAnn and Gary to make it your superpower.

How to Develop Tenacity as a Superpower

Kind and softspoken, Gary and LeAnn both used tenacity to help millions of people. When we spoke, Gary explained that tenacity was the most important lesson he'd learned in his career.

He started his nonprofit with nothing. No grant. No funds. Just an idea, he says. "You hear entrepreneurs talk about this all the time. Things always take longer than you think they're going to." His point being, only tenacity can get you through the challenges.

As a nonprofit social entrepreneur, he learned that it is difficult to "help others see the world" through the same lens he did. Still, he was motivated by the conviction that preventing unnecessary deaths from lack of access to clean water was possible. He learned that he could ultimately help people understand their ability to save lives.

His success required a good foundational idea (access to clean water saves lives) and tenacity. Here are some tips to help you build your tenacity.

1. *Find passion.* If you haven't already identified a cause you're passionate about, start there. Passion is the fuel for the tenacity engine. Gary emphasizes passion in his story.
2. *Follow role models.* Whatever cause fuels your passion, you can find people who are doing it well. Watch what they do. Emulate their best behavior. Learn from their mistakes. Channel their persistence.
3. *Don't quit.* Sometimes, people think of tenacity as simply not quitting. That's an oversimplification, but not quitting is undoubtedly an essential part of tenacity.
4. *Set goals.* Focusing on your objectives will help you keep your head up and eyes looking at the future more than the past. Write down your goals and check your progress regularly.
5. *Be fearless.* If you're working on something that matters, you will encounter challenges that scare you. Find a path to keep going.

These five tips will help you emulate LeAnn and Gary by becoming more tenacious. With effort, this could become your superpower.

Devin D. Thorpe

Part 9: Positivity

Staying positive despite immersing yourself in a problem worth solving can be challenging. For some, it is the critical difference between hoping to make a difference and actually making one. The final six chapters of the book will give you tools to help you do just that.

Marisa de Belloy

Chapter 55: Hope - Marisa de Belloy

Devin: *What is your superpower, Marisa?*

Marisa: *My superpower is keeping hope in the face of a very difficult situation, maintaining hope, coming to work every morning, helping people to do more, bringing people together, and just helping us all to move forward.*

You can watch the full interview with Marisa here: marisa.s4g.biz.

Marisa de Belloy is the executive director of the High Tide Foundation, which supports the nonprofit Cool Effect, where she previously served as CEO (for a time wearing both hats). Cool Effect focuses on rapidly addressing climate change.

Marisa led Cool Effect through a critical growth phase in scaling up charitable contributions to fight climate change. The nonprofit aggregated tested interventions structured to make meaningful, measurable carbon reductions. These measurements allow for people to donate to philanthropic causes knowing how much carbon each one eliminates. It is a carbon offset marketplace for ordinary people and charitably minded environmentalists.

Carbon offsets or carbon credits are payments carbon emitters make to other people to reduce their carbon emissions. Reducing carbon is cheaper in some circumstances than in others. So, it sometimes makes sense for emitters to pay others to cut their emissions rather than cut their own.

Cool Effect is a crowdfunding site. You visit and browse carbon reduction projects the way you might review new product ideas on

Kickstarter or people and families in crisis on GoFundMe. I can't find any that don't have social benefits in addition to environmental ones.

That connection between climate change and human beings is what drew Marisa to the work. Earlier in her career, she focused on human rights. As her career progressed, coincidentally, alongside advancing global warming, she began to feel that the climate crisis was driving challenges to human rights. Ultimately, she concluded the most impactful thing she could do for humans was to lead the charge to reverse climate change.

Corporations have funded some ineffective projects through carbon credit markets. Failures bring some negative attention to carbon offset markets. However, the reality is no different than any other sector. Some projects work better than others. Those listed on Cool Effect are literally triple verified for efficacy.

Carbon offsets effectively accelerate a global transition to a carbon-free economy. Without them, things will slow dramatically. Here's why: it makes sense to send money to the places where it will do the most good. A family could reasonably decide to spend $25,000 on solar panels to reduce its carbon footprint by ten tons every year for the next 25 years, about $100 per ton. If donated via Cool Effect, it would have more than ten times the impact for the same price. As you can see, carbon credits do play a critical role in reversing climate change.

The reality is that some of the projects on Cool Effect are so efficient, an environmentally-focused family of four with a modest carbon footprint could offset its carbon footprint for $20 per month. Few people can't afford to do that much.

The best solution, Marisa believes, is for people to do all they possibly can to eliminate their personal carbon footprint and also donate through Cool Effect to reduce carbon further, going beyond offsetting their own carbon footprint.

Living in Northern California, Marisa has seen firsthand some of the devastating effects of the climate crisis in her community. She's seen wildfires and drought alternate with floods from torrential rains. She is keenly aware of climate science, the data which suggests that we're not doing enough to avoid 1.5 or 2.0 degrees of warming. Without that progress, the weather will worsen, and the impacts will leave some populated parts of the globe effectively uninhabitable.

She sees it. She knows it. She understands it.

And she is hopeful. Her hope helps her get up every morning to do more to reverse global warming. It prevents her from quitting when the going is tough. It inspires others to persevere. On the other hand, despair defeats motivation. Hope creates it.

You can make hope your superpower, too.

How to Develop Hope as a Superpower

Marisa is working on what many agree is the biggest challenge humankind faces today. Such a big issue is daunting at times. Hope is a critical component in facing such obstacles.

Whatever issues you face, they likely feel daunting at times. If you are working to help people individually or in groups, you've undoubtedly seen that they have free will. They don't always make the choices you'd like. In other words, helping them can feel as daunting as climate change seems to Marisa. You can channel hope to help you in your work, too.

Psychologist Karen Hall, building on the work of famed Dr. Martin Seligman, whose discovery of "learned helplessness" led to the creation of a new field known as positive psychology, presented a list of six tips for catalyzing hope.[15]

1. *Get clarity.* Simplify the problem you see to strip away some of the distractions. Clarity will inherently make you feel that what you're working to accomplish is more realistic.
2. *Follow role models.* People have solved many of the world's problems. Eradicating polio is almost unbelievably frustrating and expensive. Remembering that smallpox has been eradicated provides a foundation for believing polio can be, too. No one has solved climate change, but global carbon emissions peaked in 2015, and US carbon emissions peaked in 2007. Progress may be too slow, but there is progress to acknowledge and build on. Look for role models working close to you.
3. *Do what you can.* Most problems that changemakers like you tackle can't be solved quickly. Set interim progress goals for yourself that are reasonable and attainable. Be sure to include some that are achievable based primarily on your effort. For instance, if you're raising money for a cause, the money donors provide is up to them, but the number of calls you make is entirely within your control. Setting goals of both sorts challenges you and ensures that you routinely achieve some wins, strengthening your hope muscle.
4. *Be kind.* Working on challenging projects means that you'll face setbacks and disappointments. You'll likely feel discouraged when that happens. One trick for overcoming the sense of despair you may encounter is to do something kind for someone else. It will trigger the natural release of serotonin which has an antidepressant effect.

---

[15] April 19, 2015, Karen Hall, Ph.D., Psychology Today, "Finding Hope," https://www.psychologytoday.com/us/blog/pieces-mind/201504/finding-hope.

5. *Exercise your faith.* Many belief systems guide adherents to trust in a power or being capable of overcoming significant challenges. If yours does, leverage that faith to help you over every hurdle.
6. *Practice mindfulness.* When you are discouraged by events or just a lack of progress, practice mindfulness. There are quality free and low-cost guides to help you. Many start with the simple act of focusing on your breathing. That can provide an almost instant boost of calm that will help you shift your mindset away from despair toward hope.

Following these six tips can help you develop the hope you need to keep working in the face of daunting challenges, just like Marisa. Hope can be your superpower.

Slava Rubin

Chapter 56: Optimism - Slava Rubin

Devin: *Slava, what's your superpower?*

Slava: *My superpower. That's an interesting question. I would say it is being optimistic, trying to believe that anything is possible as long as you just continue to take steps forward and learn. Yeah, that's what I would say.*

You can watch the full interview with Slava here: slava.s4g.biz.

Slava Rubin is a co-founder of crowdfunding giant Indiegogo; he served as the CEO for a decade. He continues to innovate with a focus on helping entrepreneurs succeed.

Along with co-founders Danae Ringelmann and Eric Schell, one aspect of their desire was to democratize startup funding. They struggled with the screening process used by venture capitalists and recognized that many of the ideas VCs rejected had social benefits. They could also see that women and minorities weren't getting their fair share of startup funding.

Slava and the Indiegogo team created a platform for founders to reach out to current and even prospective customers for financial help, often pre-selling products that could take months or even years to produce. By working independently of the venture capital community, entrepreneurs could achieve success without them.

One favorite Indiegogo success is Solar Roadways, the cockamamie idea of an inventor in Northern Idaho whose wife suggested putting solar panels on roads. He tried to explain why it was impossible. The more he thought about it, the more he began to believe he could harden the surface to support people and vehicles. Early in the development cycle, he raised more than $2.2 million on Indiegogo. The startup is now manufacturing solar roadway tiles and installing them on roads. Without a platform for funding ideas with help from the public, the invention would not have made it out of the garage.

Indiegogo's data shows that 47 percent of the projects that exceed their funding goal are led by women, suggesting that the platform is helping to eliminate gender disparities for entrepreneurs. With more than $1.5 billion raised on the website, the founders are realizing their social impact goals at scale.

Slava remains engaged at Indiegogo. He has also launched a seed-stage venture fund called Humbition. In addition, he started an alternative investment platform called Vincent Alternative Investments that allows everyone to quickly discover a wide range of non-traditional investments, including startups raising money via equity crowdfunding.

Entrepreneurs have always seemed to me to be among the most optimistic people on the planet. It confirmed my experience to have Slava admit that it was his superpower.

Thankfully, you don't have to be an entrepreneur to make optimism your superpower.

How to Develop Optimism as a Superpower

Slava is not alone. Optimism is the most common superpower among those interviewed for this book. Believing there must be a way to do big things, solve global problems, or help people in critical need is crucial to making them happen.

Hope, which we discussed in the last chapter, is a foundational requirement for optimism. Logically, you must hope there is a way before you can begin to form the belief and actions supporting deeper optimism.

The idea that optimism is connected to better outcomes isn't just the stuff of motivational speakers. Research among psychologists has concluded that it does. Let me repeat this another way. Science says optimism improves outcomes.

In positive psychology, therapists use optimism to treat several conditions, from bereavement to depression and even PTSD.

This is a critical chapter in this book. Mark it. Highlight it. Add notes. Take time to write down what you think when you finish with this chapter.

Now, here are five essential tips from the University of Michigan to help you develop your sense of optimism.[16]

---

[16] August 31, 2020, Healthwise Staff, University of Michigan Health, "Tapping the

1. *Focus on the positive.* You are in control of your thoughts. Choose to think about the good things that happen. As you try to develop this strength, take time each day to write down the good things that happened. Even on a crummy day, good things happen. Write those down.
2. *Practice gratitude.* Make it a habit to express genuine appreciation to everyone who helps you, from holding a door, taking your fast food order or helping you at home. Expressing gratitude is especially important with those who live with you. Take a moment toward the end of each day to thank the people who you may have missed—including people who served you indirectly. Send a text, a tweet or call someone to say thank you.
3. *Find the silver lining.* It is essential when bad things happen to begin looking for the good aspects. It could have been worse. There are lessons to learn. Some good will come from the experience. It is also healthy to experience and feel pain and sorrow when bad things happen. Optimists limit the time devoted to suffering and then move forward, focused on the silver lining.
4. *Look forward.* Envision your ultimate success at completing the project or solving the problem. You are entitled to imagine the rewards of that effort. See the happy faces of the people whose lives you may touch. Think of the time you'll take with your family when this effort is complete.
5. *Build yourself up.* To strengthen your optimism, you need to believe in yourself. Think about adding daily affirmations to your digital calendar on a repeating basis. Set one you see daily or seven you see once each week or up to 31 you see repeated once each month. Set up your calendar to send you a reminder email for these events, so you get an email every morning reminding you of your superpowers.

If you're already optimistic, some of these steps may feel unnecessary—try them anyway. If you're not inclined to optimism naturally, you may be skeptical. Developing genuine optimism is easy in that constantly doing the things on the list above will work. The vital part of that sentence is constancy. You can't develop a genuinely optimistic frame by doing this for a day or week. Make it a point to do this for at least a year. If you do, you will change your life, and you will have better outcomes. It could become your most powerful strength, your defining superpower.

Power of Optimism," https://www.uofmhealth.org/health-library/abl0330.

Khushboo Jain

Chapter 57: Optimism and Perseverance - Khushboo Jain

Devin: *Well, Khushboo, I wonder what is your superpower?*

Khushboo: *I can talk about Piyush's superpower, and maybe he can talk about mine.*

Devin: *No, that is cheating.*

Khushboo: *I think—I'm told that sometimes I'm hopelessly optimistic about things. Now, I don't know if that is a good thing or a bad thing, but yeah, I usually do not—I don't feel like giving up. Sometimes, at the surprise of so many other people around me, they say that my ability to stick it out—my ability to persevere in a situation which most people would encourage me to sort of back out, I would still stick around. And that is what I believe makes it my superpower.*

You can watch the full interview with Khushboo here: boo.s4g.biz.

Khushboo Jain is the chief operating officer of ImpactGuru, a social enterprise she co-founded with her husband, Piyush Jain (see Chapter 32). You'll recall that the company is a crowdfunding platform used primarily to fund expensive health interventions for tens of thousands of people.

Her work saves lives.

For example, Ahanti Shahane was diagnosed with dilated cardiomyopathy at just five months of age. For years, doctors treated her successfully with medicine. She enrolled in school and was an exemplary student.

By age eight, the symptoms recurred. Her parents repeatedly had to rush her to the hospital for emergency treatment. The cost of the treatments wiped the family out financially. Soon, it became clear her only hope for survival was an immediate heart transplant her family could ill afford. The total cost was over $41,000—a bargain by US standards but far out of reach for most families in India.

Her father posted her story on ImpactGuru, and 738 donors quickly donated the needed funds. She received her new heart.

Not every story is that dramatic, but many are. Khushboo and Piyush are working to integrate ImpactGuru into the healthcare system, so people aren't denied treatment but are instead helped to fundraise. To ensure that patients in dire straits both financially and physically are not left on their own, Doctors and hospitals participate in the fundraising process.

Creating and growing a remarkable social enterprise where failure could mean death in so many cases, Khushboo keeps going. She doesn't even feel like quitting. She attributes her perseverance to her unfailing optimism.

You can combine optimism and perseverance into your own superpower.

How to Develop Optimism and Perseverance as a Superpower

Helping to lead ImpactGuru would, at least at times, feel more like working in the healthcare industry than in the tech sector. Khushboo faces life and death every day. Imagine being so resilient that she never feels like giving up.

Have you ever felt like giving up? I have. Most people have.

As mentioned in Chapter 56, research has established that optimism improves outcomes. Improved perseverance is likely to contribute to that, as Khushboo demonstrates. Superpowers tend to reinforce one another, making it possible for you to develop several as personal strengths.

Here are three ways to use your optimism to help you become more persevering.

1. *See solutions.* When problems arise, to avoid feeling like quitting— to channel your inner Khushboo—focus on solutions. Your optimism will give you confidence that you can solve problems. You can solve the current crisis.

2. *Identify capacity.* Dedicated runners see hills to run up as challenges that strengthen them. Your optimism will help you see difficulties the same way. Not only will your positive attitude help you find your inner strength, but it will also help you see abilities in your team and community. You'll remember that you are not alone. Together, you can overcome anything.

3. *Recover quickly.* Your optimism can also help you get back up after you fall. No, your optimism won't prevent falls. But it will help you get up quickly afterward. The faster you are back on your feet, the closer you are to Khushboo, never even wanting to quit.

Doing good more often resembles a marathon than a sprint. There are times you may find yourself sprinting, but you're likely still in the middle of the race. Solving problems like those outlined in the UN Sustainable Development Goals takes time measured in years and decades rather than hours or days.

In the context of working toward goals of such magnitude, you will encounter setbacks and challenges. Your optimism is a vital tool in manifesting your perseverance. Together, optimism and perseverance are unstoppable superpowers.

Gail McGovern

Chapter 58: Optimism and Team Building - Gail McGovern

Devin: *What is your superpower?*

Gail: *My superpower?*

I think I actually have two superpowers.

One is the one we talked about. I just find good people and make sure they're smart. I make sure they're nice. I make sure there's chemistry. I make sure they get along well together. I make sure they're diverse thinkers. So I'm good at amassing a team.

But I think my other superpower is that I'm kind of nauseatingly optimistic. And my husband accuses me of being a card-carrying member of the happy club. My daughter tells me I have a weird happiness baseline. It's abnormally high. I just like to feel happy and optimistic. And I model optimism here. And when you're optimistic, people get confident, and they feel like they can do even more than they can. And it's a beautiful thing, you know, in our business responding to disasters. Our mantra is "prepare for the worst and hope for the best." And believe me, we prepare for the worst. We are ready to handle three back-to-back category four hurricanes. And we had to do so in recent history. But I prepare for the worst. But I also expect the best. And when you feel that way, you do feel like you have a superpower. So I would say optimism and modeling optimism is my secret sauce, as they say.

You can watch the full interview with Gail here: gail.s4g.biz.

Gail McGovern is the CEO of the American Red Cross. In 2008, she took the position when the huge nonprofit was in debt and had been experiencing a revolving door in the CEO's office, with Gail becoming the eighth one to hold the position in just five years.

The Red Cross needed a leader. She's still there because she is one.

She led the organization through its challenges and enabled the Red Cross to respond effectively to Hurricane Sandy in 2012 and Hurricanes Harvey, Irma and Maria in 2017.

Those headline-grabbing disasters represent a relatively small part of what the Red Cross does. Each year the organization responds to tens of thousands of tragedies, primarily single-family home fires. The organization also helps to maintain the country's blood supply and supports our military and their families.

While Gail got the job because she is a strong leader, she was remarkably open with me about what she had learned about leadership during her tenure.

"After 28 years in the for-profit world, you would think I had learned what I need to learn," Gail said. Referring to her experience leading the Red Cross, she added, "But it taught me to be a different and better leader as a result of that experience."

Gail shared what she learned about being a leader, lessons she says would have applied perfectly in her for-profit experience to make her a better leader.

"Back when I was in the for-profit sector, you know, I would tell people, 'Calm down. It's just telecommunications. We're not saving lives here,' or at Fidelity, I'd say, 'Calm down. You know, it's just managing money. We're not saving lives here," she explains. "That schtick doesn't work at the American Red Cross."

"What I've learned at the Red Cross is it's possible to not only lead with your head but also lead with your heart." She now wishes she'd brought more passion to her work at AT&T and Fidelity.

Her optimism and team-building capabilities are her superpowers. You can make them yours, too.

How to Develop Optimism and Team Building as Superpowers

Gail's extraordinary leadership style incorporates her optimism and team building. Elsewhere in this book, we've explored some vital leadership principles and optimism. Now, you can focus on the intersection to think about how optimism influences your ability to build a strong team.

Gail describes her team building as a function of hiring the right people, making sure they're "smart," "nice" and have "chemistry" with the rest of the team. She describes her optimism as something she "models" as a leader, "When you're optimistic, people get confident, and they feel like they can do even more than they can."

She must also use her optimism to help her recruit smart, nice people. People are more attracted to optimists than pessimists, allowing her to recruit her target hires.

Research is clear that optimists make better leaders.[17] An optimistic leadership style helps to create a more cooperative environment, which is especially important, Gail says, in a nonprofit. Optimism also translates to greater empowerment for others in the organization. This appears to result from optimistic leaders giving their people more latitude given the leader's confidence in their success and, as Gail explained, giving people greater confidence in themselves.

Here are three simple ways to incorporate optimism into your leadership.

1. *Communicate optimism.* Be deliberate about communicating optimism to your team. In a crisis, when it counts most, your ability to reassure people that you can overcome the problems together could be the difference between success and failure.
2. *Set realistic goals.* Nothing will drain optimism from your team faster than repeatedly failing to hit targets. Work with them to develop reasonable, challenging goals that you can reach together at least some of the time. If your team always hits the target, you may need to push a bit harder.
3. *Model successful failure.* Optimists get better results, but that doesn't mean they never fail. As a leader, when you struggle, you need to model remarkable optimism. Own your mistakes.

---

[17] Prof. (Dr.) Shyamalendu Niyogi, Impact of Optimism on Leadership Effectiveness: A Review of Literature. International Journal of Management, 8 (6), 2017, pp. 1–8. http://iaeme.com/Home/issue/IJM?Volume=8&Issue=6.

Demonstrate your willingness to learn from challenges and move forward quickly.

These three practices will help you incorporate optimism into your leadership style.

By doing so, you can be a leader more like Gail. Optimism and team building can become your superpowers.

Chapter 59: Positivity - Josh Tickell

Devin: *What is your superpower?*

Josh: *Well, I think part of my superpower is, you know, you asked me why did I dive in and do those things I did. And I think there's a part of my superpower that's memory loss or naivete. You know I keep thinking that "Oh, this one will be much easier; this time, it's going to be much better." So I forget the struggle. And I get into the sort of fantasy or the great feeling of like how's the future going to be when we accomplish that. And to some degree, that's good because if all we remember is the difficulty and the struggle, we never accomplish big things. So part of my superpower is forgetting all the negativity and tuning out the negativity that other people have because I'm in my 40s. I have two children. My wife and I work together on our films and our projects. People go, "Well, that's never going to work, you can never–" It's a lot more common now that we're grownups than when we were kids. And I just tune it out. I'm just like, you're just on the wrong radio dial, you're just on the wrong frequency for me. So, part of my superpower is just being able to focus on the positive stuff, the positive possibility.*

You can watch the full interview with Josh here: josh.s4g.biz.

Josh Tickell is a documentary filmmaker and author who has focused his prolific career on the environment. His most recent projects are book and movie pairs, *Kiss the Ground* and *The Revolution Generation*.

Josh's work for *Kiss the Ground* features a meaningful part of a revolution in agriculture, moving toward a regenerative approach that requires less water, less fertilizer, fewer pesticides and, most remarkably, sequesters carbon. Its impact is sufficient to reverse climate change. It also restores, protects, and even creates topsoil rather than accelerating its being washed and blown away by conventional farming.

As a vegan myself, I was fascinated by what he taught me about cows. Cattle and other animals contribute to climate change in well-documented ways. Cows famously belch vast amounts of methane, for instance. It turns out, however, that when farmers raise cows in an organic, regenerative setting, they play a critical role in working their waste into the soil, serving as a potent fertilizer, improving the soil's ability to retain water, nutrients and carbon. Without animals, the system doesn't achieve these results.

Josh's work is inherently problematic. Even bestselling authors and filmmakers struggle at times. His film *Fuel*, which documented the growth of biofuels, became an international sensation. The well-deserved attention came, in part, because the film also captured the decline of biofuels, which is sadly representative of the direction the world has moved since.

Dealing with the challenges inherent in independent filmmaking, like raising money and finding distribution, highlights Josh's superpower of positivity. It may go without saying that without it, he couldn't have accomplished all he has.

How to Develop Positivity as a Superpower

During my recent Congressional campaign, which was the most challenging thing I'd done in my career, a dear friend and psychologist, Dr. Paul Jenkins, offered to coach me through the campaign to keep me positive. He wrote the book *Pathological Positivity*. Dr. Paul helped me channel my inner Josh Tickell during the campaign.

Josh may have a natural ability to ignore the negative and see the positive, but you can learn to do it, too. No matter how challenging things get, there are practices Dr. Paul has taught me—and millions of others—that will help you find your inner Josh.

The following tips, extracted from Dr. Paul's book, will help you be more positive.

1. *Drive.* You are the driver. You can control your thoughts and your emotions more than you may realize. You make countless decisions every day without thinking about them. You experience more without noticing. Stop, right now. What language are you reading? Have you thought about the fact you're reading English even once today? If it's your native language, the answer is likely "no." How does your shirt feel on your skin? Have you thought about that today? Your subconscious brain is busy, but you are the driver. So drive!

2. *Remember, it could be worse.* When something challenging in life happens, it's natural to think about how things were better before they happened. That is a negative, even if typical, frame. You can instead think about how it could have been worse. So you fall and break a leg. That is terrible. No doubt. What if you had hit your head instead? Could you be dead? When you put your current situation in a frame next to "it could have been worse," you already start to feel better. (Note: use this counsel on yourself, not your friends. Empathy demands you not make less of others' suffering.)

3. *Focus on solutions.* When a problem arises, it is helpful to begin thinking about what could make the situation better. Think first about outcomes with the issue resolved, corrected or overcome. Next, give some thought to the actions required to make that reality. As you focus on solutions, you are becoming more positive. You are channeling your inner Josh Tickell.

4. *Take action immediately.* Don't get overwhelmed by the effort required to solve the entire problem. Give yourself a short deadline, like 8:00 tonight or tomorrow morning. Ask yourself what you could do between now and then to solve the problem. What you do could be something small, tiny, in fact. The key is to identify something you can do almost immediately and then do it. Taking action feels empowering and will help you create your internal positivity.

5. *Keep it up.* Dr. Paul suggests that you try to make it a habit to do something every day to improve things, once before 8:00 am and again before 8:00 pm. Personally, I think noon and midnight work better, but the idea is the same. Twice each day, make it a point to do something that moves you closer to a better place. As that becomes habitual, you should see your positivity become more consistent as well.

Josh likely does a lot of this, though he may never have worked through the steps with Dr. Paul or anyone else. He does see how it could be worse and shifts his mental energy to solutions and actions to overcome the challenges. It's habitual, and it works.

By learning from Dr. Paul, you can be more like Josh. You can make positivity your superpower. If negativity constrains your success, just making a bit of positivity progress can change your life and your impact.

Bill Gates by Matt Slotemaker

Chapter 60: Patience and Optimism - Bill Gates

Devin: *A few years ago, you wrote about superpowers in your annual letter. What is your superpower?*

Bill: *Well, if I have one, it has something to do with optimism about scientific innovation and being able to gather teams of people. My experience at Microsoft was assembling teams of engineers and understanding what was on track/off track, being patient for things that, in that case, usually took five or six years. In the world of medicine, unfortunately, it's like ten years. The HIV vaccine–between when people started working on it and when we'll finally have one–that will have been almost 25 years. So the patience required, the need to have multiple strategies, so it's there in pushing for innovations.*

And then directing the resources that I'm lucky enough to have both through Microsoft and that Warren Buffett has made available. Thank goodness it's allowed us to be ambitious, including the scale we're at on polio. Warren was just in Seattle this week, and I was saying to him, "Hey,

Pakistan—a few setbacks." And he said, "You gotta keep going. You know, it's great that you're doing this."

You can watch the full interview with Bill here: gates.s4g.biz.

Bill Gates, founder of Microsoft and co-chair of the Bill and Melinda Gates Foundation, was, for nearly a generation, the wealthiest person on the planet. Among billionaires, he has been the role model for genuine philanthropy. Using the Giving Pledge, he has advocated for donating the majority of one's wealth to solving society's most pressing problems.

He personally executes this pledge through his foundation. The Gates Foundation is the largest private foundation in the world. For years, its most significant funding commitment has been to the eradication of polio. While the end of polio will not be celebrated in 2021, there are early signs that the last case of wild poliovirus could be this year. As of this writing, there have been just two cases in the entire world, one each in Afghanistan and Pakistan.

The bigger problem now is the number of circulating vaccine-derived poliovirus (cVDPV) cases. One in several million immunizations using the Albert Sabin oral polio vaccine mutates, and a child catches or becomes contagious with the disease. In communities with low vaccination rates, polio spreads. In 2021, there have been dozens of cVDPV cases.

This problem highlights the contribution of the Gates Foundation. Under Bill's active leadership, the Gates Foundation began work a decade ago on a new oral vaccine that cannot mutate to cause even a single case of polio.

At the time, India, which many had expected to be the last country with polio cases, appeared to have eradicated the disease. A few years later, that result was confirmed. So, as the Gates Foundation was talking about developing a new polio vaccine that might not be ready for use for a decade, many thought it would never be needed because the disease would be eradicated before a new vaccine could be approved.

Fast forward, and the incredible foresight is clear. The Gates Foundation and its partners in the Global Polio Eradication Initiative (Rotary International, the World Health Organization, UNICEF, the U.S. Centers for Disease Control and the Global Vaccine Alliance) are now deploying the novel vaccine to replace the traditional Sabin oral vaccine.

The novel vaccine could be the only way to stop the spread of polio as immunization rates fall in countries that haven't had a case of polio in years or even decades. In such places, one mutated vaccination can start an outbreak. The novel vaccine shepherded by Bill himself will be the linchpin to polio eradication.

The novel vaccine is also a great example of Bill using his superpowers: optimism and patience. His particular brand of optimism focused on his ability to move the vaccine process forward quickly enough to play a role in eradication while at the same time having the patience to work on it for a decade.

Following Bill's example, you can make optimism and patience your superpowers, too.

How to Develop Optimism and Patience as Superpowers

Bill's optimism and patience have helped make the world a better place, especially for the millions of children who would have contracted polio had he not worked to prevent it. You can develop the same superpowers.

In Chapter 56 with Slava Rubin, you read about how to develop optimism as a superpower. Here, you will read how to use your optimism to strengthen your patience and how patience can amplify and expand all your superpowers.

Operating with the view that your efforts will bring desired results makes patience easier to manifest. Good things always seem to take longer than expected, but remaining hopeful helps you keep working for the outcomes you want. Bill worked for a decade on the new vaccine, hoping it would arrive in time to be of help in the fight to eradicate polio. Thank heaven he did.

Psychologist Paul Jenkins has some ideas for developing patience that I've adapted for this chapter.[18]

1. *Think about your thinking.* Developing patience requires you to think about the fact that you have some control over your thinking. You can observe your thoughts and feelings, the inner dialog in your head. (Psychologists call this metacognition.) Not only can you monitor what's happening in your mind, but you can also change it.
2. *See your expectations.* Now that you are in your head, you can see how things that cause you to feel disappointed, frustrated or impatient often happen because what is happening doesn't align with your expectations around timing. Some people who will camp overnight, waiting for the first chance to buy a new consumer product, get frustrated waiting a few minutes for fast food. It is not the wait that causes the problem; it is the expectation that fast food

---

[18] November 14, 2019, Dr. Paul Jenkins, Vicki Jenkins, "How To Be Patient In A Relationship," https://youtu.be/1ChbBVknKD4.

should come faster. Look at how your expectations about your progress may be contributing to your impatience.

3. *Assess the now.* Recognizing that you may not be where you'd hoped, and that may have important implications, ask yourself if it is too late? Bill hoped the vaccine would be available sooner but could see its future value. Progress may have been slower than expected, but it was not too late. The novel vaccine may hold the key to polio eradication.

4. *Inventory your progress.* Take a moment in your pain to reflect on the progress you've made, the skills you've learned and the people you have helped. If you have been working to address a significant social problem, you'll have something to show for it, even if it is primarily a better understanding of the challenge.

5. *Accept what is.* Understanding that you aren't where you hoped to be, you can choose to accept that reality. The choice to accept the situation can be a conscious one that helps relieve the pain you're feeling.

6. *Change your expectations.* You don't need to give up on your goals, but there may be times during your journey to impact when you have to recognize that you aren't where you expected to be. Recalibrate. Change your expectations. This adjustment will contribute to a sense of relief and allow you to move forward.

7. *Keep working.* One final step to help you overcome feelings of impatience is to keep working. Taking action is empowering. Once you've completed the steps above, do something to move you toward your ultimate goal.

With patience, you have a superpower that strengthens every other superpower in the book. Learning to move forward patiently will improve your tenacity and persistence. It will reflect on your optimism, allowing you to be hopeful even when others despair. By giving yourself time to develop any of the superpowers in this book, you enable yourself to conquer more of them.

Remember, some of the superpowers in the book may be yours to master. Others may illuminate a weakness that limits your success. With effort and time, you can eliminate such shortcomings. No one has all 60 superpowers described in this book. Not even Bill. Following his example, pairing optimism and patience, can enable you to do more in the long run than you ever imagined.

Devin Thorpe by Kelsey Farley

About the Author

Devin is a bestselling author who calls himself a champion of social good. He ran for Congress in 2020. Drawing on more than 1,200 interviews with changemakers, he loves to share stories of their "superpowers for good." As a Forbes contributor, with over 500 bylines and over two million unique readers, he became a recognized name in the social impact arena. His YouTube show and podcast, featuring celebrities, CEOs, billionaires, entrepreneurs—including Bill Gates—and others who are out to change the world, gave him a recognizable face as well.

His books, focusing on helping readers do more good in the world, have been read over 1 million times!

He has helped nonprofits raise millions of dollars via crowdfunding. He twice hosted a 24-hour livestream via YouTube on #GivingTuesday, featuring more than 90 interviews with nonprofit leaders.

Previously, Devin served as the CFO of the third-largest company on the 2009 Inc. 500 list. He also founded and led a FINRA-registered investment bank. After completing a degree in finance at the University of Utah, he earned an MBA from Cornell University.

Having lived on three continents and visited over 40 countries on six continents and with guests from around the world on his show, Devin brings a global perspective on purpose-driven leadership to international audiences–from the UN to Nepal–empowering them to do more good and make their mark on the world. These lessons also enable them to change their personal lives and to drive positive change within their organizations.

Today, Devin channels the idealism of his youth, volunteering whenever and wherever he can, with the loving support of his wife, Gail.

Devin D. Thorpe

Their son, Dayton Thorpe, Ph.D. works in San Francisco. Frequently finding himself on airplanes, Devin is glad to be middle-seat-sized.

Also by Devin D. Thorpe

Subscribe to the Superpowers for Good newsletter at *devinthorpe.substack.com*.

Your Mark on the World: Stories of service that show us how to give more with a purpose without giving up what's most important.

925 Ideas to Help You Save Money, Get Out of Debt and Retire a Millionaire So You Can Leave Your Mark on the World

Crowdfunding for Social Good: Financing Your Mark on the World

Adding Profit by Adding Purpose: The CFO's Corporate Social Responsibility Handbook